The Minimum Level of Unemployment and Public Policy

Frank C. Pierson
Swarthmore College

THE W.E. UPJOHN INSTITUTE FOR EMPLOYMENT RESEARCH

Library of Congress Cataloging in Publication Data

Pierson, Frank Cook, 1911-
  The minimum level of unemployment and public policy.

  1. Unemployment—United States. 2. United States—
Full employment policies. I. Title.
HD5724.P475   339.5'0973   80-26536
ISBN 0-911558-76-4
ISBN 0-911558-75-6 (pbk.)

iii

The Author

Professor Pierson has devoted most of his professional career to teaching and research work in the labor field, along with various government and arbitration assignments in the same area. He joined the Economics Department of Swarthmore College in 1940, served as Vice-Chairman of the Third Regional War Labor Board during World War II, subsequently was a research associate at various universities and institutes and was active both as an arbitrator in private industry and as a consultant to several government agencies. He is Joseph Wharton Professor Emeritus of Political Economy at Swarthmore College.

He is the author of a variety of studies in the labor and manpower field including *Community Wage Patterns*, 1952; *New Concepts in Wage Determination* (co-editor), 1957; *The Education of American Businessmen* (with others), 1959; and *Community Manpower Training Programs for the Disadvantaged*, 1972.

Foreword

While the problem of cyclical joblessness dominates public policy discussion at the present time, structural unemployment is being increasingly recognized as one of the nation's most serious domestic problems. Persistent high levels of "prosperity" or structural unemployment are attributable to seemingly intractable structural imbalances within the economy. As Professor Pierson notes, the key policy problem centers on the use of aggregative and structural policies to reduce total unemployment to the 4-5 percent range and to bring the hard-to-employ into the economic mainstream without inducing increased inflation.

This study focuses on the role of the federal government in reducing persistent joblessness that prevails at relatively high levels even during periods of high employment or prosperity. Professor Pierson concludes that, while differing in degree, both cyclical and structural unemployment should be addressed in periods of high as in periods of low employment. The author concludes that the most critical issue to resolve is how to balance short-run and long-run goals for the economy in the selection of public policy alternatives.

Facts and observations expressed in the study are the sole responsibility of the author. His viewpoints do not necessarily represent positions of the W.E. Upjohn Institute for Employment Research.

E. Earl Wright
Director

Kalamazoo, Michigan
November 1980

Contents

Chapter 1
Dimensions of the Problem

In the last decade, unemployment has again become one of the country's most serious unresolved problems. Mass unemployment as it was known in the 1930s can perhaps no longer be considered a serious threat, an outcome for which Keynes and his followers deserve primary credit. The full employment prospect implicit in their doctrines, however, has faded. The broad consensus among economists today is that if reliance is placed on Keynesian macro-expansion policies alone, the jobless rate cannot be pushed below 5 percent, perhaps not even below 6 percent, of the nation's labor force without unleashing severe inflationary pressures.

Compared to the Great Depression such projections hardly appear alarming, but the economic and social repercussions of even small changes in the jobless rate can be extremely serious. A rise in the jobless rate of one percentage point, say from 4 to 5 percent, would add about a million persons to the jobless rolls and, barring temporary offsets, would reduce real GNP by nearly 3 percent. More serious still, the kind of unemployment that persists into periods of general prosperity falls much more heavily on certain groups than on others: those with low incomes, few skills, and little education. In addition to the loss of their output, society must also bear the heavy direct and indirect costs of the added welfare expenditures, police protection, and

1

neighborhood deterioration associated with concentrated joblessness of this type. Most damaging of all, persons who cannot even find stable jobs in boom periods can hardly be blamed for becoming completely discouraged and defeatist about their personal worth as well as their role in the life of their communities.

This study is primarily addressed to the problem of prosperity, as opposed to recessionary, unemployment. The former is attributable to persistent structural imbalances within the economy, the latter to either cyclical or longer term shortfalls in aggregate demand relative to aggregate supply in the economy as a whole. The distinction between structural and aggregate demand joblessness has admittedly become quite blurred since failure on either front greatly complicates effective action on the other. To the degree aggregate imbalances prove intractable, structural imbalances will become more serious, and if the latter prove to be unyielding, the task of aggregate demand management becomes correspondingly more difficult. Parallel action on both fronts is, therefore, clearly required if success on either is to be achieved. Nevertheless, the corrective measures to be taken at the structural and aggregative level will differ radically.

Prosperity Unemployment

Controversy soon emerges when discussion of these two aspects of unemployment goes beyond the level of generalization. The crux of the question is how can aggregative and structural policies be meshed so that unemployment can be brought down to the 4 - 5 percent range. The usual answer is that, on the aggregative level, the economy has become increasingly inflation prone and, on the structural level, larger sections of the nation's labor force have become increasingly cut off from stable job or career opportunities. The main purpose of this study is to assess the merits of this pessimistic but widely accepted view and, more particularly, to examine its implications for public policy.

The pessimists' view has now become part of the conventional wisdom, so much so that only the briefest summary is needed here. If, as recent experience attests, prices begin to rise sharply even when the unemployment rate is as high as 6 percent or more, the scope left to fiscal and monetary policy as a means for reducing unemployment will be sharply reduced. Indeed, to the extent serious inflation has become permanent and essentially irreversible over a given two- or three-year period, any effort to lower unemployment by expansionary fiscal-monetary means will, in this view, tend in the longer run to raise rather than lower the jobless rate.

The alternative approach to the prosperity unemployment problem, directly attacking major structural barriers to jobs, has led to a hardly less pessimistic conclusion. While differing in emphasis and specific findings, the conclusion of most investigations is that the many public and private efforts since the early 1960s to remove such barriers have yielded but the barest results. The main differences among these investigations depend on the weight which is placed on improving existing job market conditions as opposed to more far-reaching reforms, the former relying chiefly on private market processes and the latter on various types of governmental intervention. Both seem generally agreed, however, that the problem itself lies beyond any quick or even distant solution.

The upshot is that the trade-off between unemployment and price stability, the well-known Phillips Curve, is now seen to be much more adverse, not only in terms of its shape but in terms of its location as well, than when first developed in the mid-fifties—how adverse, however, remains an unsettled question, with most estimates of the minimum level to which unemployment can be reduced by aggregative and structural policies without setting off a serious rise in the inflation rate ranging from 6 percent to as low as 4 percent. The choice of public policy measures for dealing with unemployment that persists into periods of general prosperity largely turns on where the effects of fiscal-monetary expansion are assumed to fall within this range of values. The general conclusion emerging from the discussion of this issue in the following chapter is that the inflationary impact of macroeconomic measures to achieve and maintain full employment, as the latter term is usually defined, has been exaggerated and that, quite aside from efforts to remove structural barriers to employment, there is good reason to believe that the jobless rate could be reduced by such measures to 5 percent or even less without affecting the rate of inflation in any significant way.

This finding, if valid, puts the question of the structural barriers to unemployment in a quite different light from the way it is usually viewed. Since the unemployment-prone groups, consisting of lesser skilled, lesser educated workers, are especially benefitted by any general lowering of the unemployment rate, structural unemployment could be expected to fall by well over one-half if it turned out that the national jobless rate could be reduced to 5 percent by macroeconomic demand policy without incurring serious inflationary consequences. This in turn would mean that efforts to bring the hard-to-employ into the mainstream of job opportunities could be concentrated much more intensively, and presumably more successfully, on the needs of the particular groups involved. An evaluation of these efforts, considered from this perspective, constitutes the chief subject of this inquiry.

Dimensions of the Problem

The basis for the view that the unemployment problem has become largely intractable rests largely on the belief that various forms of governmental intervention, however well intentioned or even justified in any given instance, have been carried to the point where, in the aggregate, full utilization of the nation's labor force on a sustained basis has become impossible. In part, this view rests on the belief that the general role of government, particularly in its fiscal and monetary policies, has been highly unstabilizing, so much so that any short-run efforts to offset such unstabilizing effects have proved ineffective and actually exacerbating. More recently, criticism has centered on governmental interventions in individual markets or broader sectors of the economy whether aimed at protecting certain producer groups or the general public. Increasingly, investigators of both a conservative and liberal persuasion have come to question whether the net effects of governmental regulation in such fields as railroads and trucking, or its efforts to control environmental, health, and safety hazards in a variety of industries have not pushed up costs unduly, thereby serving to restrict output and employment and thus contributing to both more inflation and more unemployment.

A similar shift in sentiment has occurred among investigators of government efforts to improve the performance of particular labor markets and to protect certain vulnerable worker groups. Again, rather than stressing the beneficial aspects of such efforts, increasing emphasis has come to be placed on their deleterious effects. Some of the policies that have been most widely criticized on this score are federal laws stipulating minimum wages and maximum hours, protection of union organizing and strike actions, and provision of unemployment benefits and welfare benefits. The danger of these policies, while sometimes viewed in extreme categorical terms, is more often seen as one of degree, with the argument often turning on how far is it possible for government to go in providing special safeguards of these sorts without adversely affecting the functioning of labor markets. A major purpose of this study is to review the available evidence concerning this important issue.

While the majority of professional investigators have become increasingly skeptical about governmental aggregate demand policies and individual market approaches to the problem of prosperity unemployment, an important minority hold to the view that the problem of persistent unemployment can be traced not to particular government policies but to various fundamental changes in the economy. At the aggregate level it is argued by members of this minority group that pressures arising from international economic imbalances, domestic interest group demands, changes in market trends and requirements, and shifts in factor supply conditions have made it more difficult to maintain noninflationary expansions. At the individual market level it is argued further that certain employees, most notably teenage minority workers in inner cities and the least skilled, least educated workers in economically depressed industries and areas, have become effectively cut off from all worthwhile job opportunities. In part, these barriers are said to be the result of deliberate discriminatory practices but in greater part they are felt to be the product of general cultural influences and long-standing institutional relationships. Proponents of this position share much of the skepticism of the majority group regarding the effectiveness of government measures to deal with the problem of persistent unemployment but for diametrically opposite reasons. The majority view is that the economy is generally capable of providing adequate job opportunities if only the government would adopt less sweeping programs and give unregulated market processes freer rein, while the minority holds that the imbalances and conflicts within the economy are so serious they will not be resolved unless there are far reaching changes in the economy.

It is not possible within the confines of this study to make an adequate appraisal of either of these polar positions since both are wide ranging in nature and pertinent data are not readily available. Rather, this investigation is limited to a review of the public policy implications of the findings of both groups of observers as judged by the record of prior efforts to deal with the problem of unemployment in periods of high employment or prosperity.[1] To this end attention first centers on identifying the more important characteristics of this type of unemployment and on setting forth the major questions that remain unanswered about it.

Four Aspects of Prosperity Unemployment

The first and probably the most important dimension of this kind of unemployment is that it is largely confined to certain groups and geographical areas. Viewed in demographic terms, joblessness in high employment periods is concentrated among youth, women, and older workers (54 years and over), particularly the nonwhite members of these groups. Viewed in locational terms, this type of unemployment is centered in certain long-depressed areas such as the Appalachian Region, and more massively in the inner areas of some of the country's larger cities. The same demographic groups are dominant in the geographical concentrations of joblessness, reflecting the more basic forces which lie behind persistent unemployment of this sort. It should be noted that adult white males can also find themselves without jobs in

---

1. In this study the terms *high employment* and *prosperity unemployment* are used interchangeably to denote the kind of persistent unemployment that continues at relatively high levels even in periods of sustained business expansions.

boom times but only in unusual or temporary cases. Thus prosperity level joblessness can be viewed as largely an age-sex-race problem, and policy proposals should be formulated accordingly.

Related to this dimension of the problem is the fact that many of these workers face severe labor market initial-entry or re-entry difficulties in getting stable, career-related jobs. The key issue, particularly in generally prosperous environments, is not one of finding a job as such, but rather one of getting work with promise of some permanence and longer term career potential. Indeed, the salient characteristic of this type of unemployment is not so much long periods of joblessness as short periods occurring between relatively brief spells of employment. Whether such highly unstable patterns of work stem from low productivity because of poor work habits and inexperience, or from discriminatory practices and institutional arrangements, or even from personal life styles and preferences of the workers themselves, it is clear that the most critical difficulties in dealing with prosperity level unemployment occur when workers initially enter or re-enter the labor market. For many, indeed the great majority, steady work is eventually found, albeit with a trial and error period of "shopping around" often involved; but for a substantial minority, steady work in anything approaching a career framework is not attained. These are the workers in the dead-end jobs who constitute the bulk of the so-called permanently unemployed (or the "permanently-temporarily" unemployed) and pose the most intractable aspect of the problem for policymakers.

Unemployment among older workers follows a quite different pattern. Once having achieved relatively permanent job status, a person typically remains at work until age 65 unless he or she chooses earlier retirement, and recently enacted federal legislation extends protection from dismissal for older workers until their seventieth year. Unemployment rates for such workers are comparatively low, generally running below 3 percent. If, however, they lose their jobs, the resulting unemployment is likely to prove of much longer duration than for younger persons.

A second dimension of the prosperity unemployment problem is that in the course of a broad business expansion an increasing percentage of the unemployed population is likely to consist of persons with loose or marginal labor force attachments. Teenagers, women, and workers with minimal skills or limited work experience tend to move in and out of the job market much more frequently than other worker groups, entering the labor market in relatively greater numbers in upswings and leaving in relatively greater numbers when job market conditions turn less favorable. To the extent this two-way movement occurs, it serves to hold up the overall unemployment rate in expansions and lower it in contractions. It also means that the unemployment that persists into expansion periods will increasingly consist of persons close to the margin between looking and not looking for work. While hard to quantify, it is obvious that this aspect of prosperity unemployment requires much more selective policy approaches than the type of unemployment that is predominant in periods of contraction.

Among workers close to the working-nonworking margin, two general categories call for special attention by policymakers: those who can readily find stable jobs or can take the necessary steps to qualify for such jobs if they choose to do so, as opposed to those who for personal or other reasons beyond their control cannot. The well-educated, experienced job seeker who is the second breadwinner in a family clearly requires quite different assistance, if indeed any is required at all, from the poorly educated, inexperienced job seeker who is the sole breadwinner in a low income, nonwhite family. Within each of these two categories, as discussed more fully later, other subgroupings need to be recognized. One of the important tasks of policymakers is to identify the various groups involved more carefully and fashion policy measures appropriate to each.

A third dimension of the prosperity unemployment problem, which bears directly on the one just noted, is the increased emphasis that needs to be placed in periods of broad expansion on job opportunities in the private as opposed to the public sector. It is in such periods that the private sector, which in any event normally provides about 80 percent of all jobs, is in the best position to train and take on hard-to-employ workers. It is in such periods that private employers will be most likely to have unfilled vacancies in the higher paying, more desirable lines of work. The public sector can be expected to continue its role of maintaining essential training of certain low skilled workers and of providing jobs on at least a temporary basis for such workers, but the principal aim of policy would need to shift to inducing private firms to take on workers from the hard-to-employ category. This is a critically important positive factor because it means that normal market processes can be relied on to achieve most of the tasks of bringing excluded, unemployment-prone workers into the mainstream of employment opportunities. The major difficulty besetting efforts in this direction in periods of business slack is that the job needs of employers are too limited to make effective action possible, with new placements to a considerable extent simply taking the place of other economically vulnerable groups of workers. As labor supply conditions tighten, however, the focus of policy can shift from the much more difficult objective of creating new job openings to facilitating the training-recruiting process of filling already existing openings. It would be naive to argue from this that the plight of the jobless can be largely forgotten in periods of general prosperity, but it would be equally unrealistic to formulate a set of policies that does not take this as its central starting point.

Within the public sector itself an analogous shift in policy away from federal to state and local government employment would also be appropriate in periods of sustained expansion. Opportunities for stable work in such periods are more likely to be concentrated at the local rather than national government level. Federal direction and support would still be needed but implementation would be required at the individual community, or even individual neighborhood, level. This would in turn mean placing even more responsibility on local public sponsors and administrative units than is provided under present federal legislation, however difficult the meshing of centralized and decentralized requirements is likely to be.

A fourth dimension is that the job needs of workers remaining unemployed even in generally prosperous times will not be met unless both they and their potential employers are induced to participate in broadened hiring and training programs in response to specific incentives and penalties. The type of economic and social behavior sought cannot be achieved by invoking appeals to conscience or the mere likelihood of eventual success. The advantages and disadvantages of the proposed patterns of action must be seen to be reasonably immediate, clear, and assured to both the participating workers and the employers; otherwise, the kind of sustained response necessary for the success of the program cannot be expected. This requirement for effective action, however, conflicts with another equally important requirement: since the factors giving rise to the problem of prosperity unemployment are deeply imbedded in the society's economic and social institutions, the results of even the best conceived policies are apt to be quite long delayed. Perhaps the most important issue facing policymakers in this area is how this conflict in requirements can be reconciled or at least substantially modified.

These four dimensions, along with the aggregate relationships adverted to earlier, constitute the principal considerations which need to be kept in focus in evaluating proposals for bringing down the basic or minimum unemployment rate in this country. Other considerations will be touched on at later points: the rapid increase during strong expansion periods in the labor force participation rates of certain groups in the population (including illegal aliens!); the lessons from English, Swedish and other European countries' experiences; and the importance of such "indirect" approaches as improved investment incentives, area development programs, and lowered barriers to product market competition. Main attention in this study, however, centers on the behavior of labor markets in periods of expanding business and on the various direct approaches which have been attempted or suggested for improving the performance of such markets. The evaluation of these approaches will turn on how effective they are in meeting the four dimensions of the problem outlined above.

Chapter 2
The Shifting Limits of
Demand Management

As in other aspects of modern life, the pace of change in economic ideas has greatly accelerated in recent years. In no other area of the subject is this more apparent than in prevailing attitudes towards unemployment. After World War II, a jobless rate of 3 percent or less was a generally agreed-upon goal. In the course of the 1950s and 1960s, a figure of 4 to 4.5 percent came to be accepted as at least an interim target. In the early 1970s, the most widely cited figure fell in the range of 5 to 5.5 percent, but the present administration, as required by the Humphrey-Hawkins Act, has set its sights on the more ambitious goal of 4 percent by 1983. To realize the latter figure would require an average annual increase in real GNP of about 4.5 percent over the intervening period, a decidedly optimistic assumption.

Similar changes have occurred in public attitudes towards a second major objective of economic policy: stability of the price level. In the early postwar period, after the inflationary outburst attendant on World War II, the idea of a zero annual rate of price increase was widely and seriously discussed. During the 1950s and early 1960s the most generally accepted goal came to be about 2 or perhaps 3 percent. Today, in the wake of Vietnam and the inflationary surge of the middle and late seventies, the target has risen to well over 4 percent even though this is the limiting figure set for 1983 by the Humphrey-Hawkins Act.

Explanatory Factors

These two objectives of economic policy have had to be scaled back over the postwar years because in both respects actual performance over this period has been generally disappointing. Except in times of war or the aftermath of war, the unemployment rate has kept above 4 percent in every year since World War II, and, more typically, at or above 5 percent. More striking still, even in the years of vigorous peacetime prosperity, the jobless rate has generally held above the 4 percent figure, remaining especially high in peacetime cyclical upswings in the late 1950s and again in the early 1970s. The annual rate of increase in consumer prices, on the other hand, has kept below 2 percent in most peacetime years during this period. It is only since 1968 that the yearly rate of increase in prices has jumped to much higher levels. Between 1974 and 1976 the rise in consumer prices fell from 12 percent to 5 percent per year, but a move back towards a much higher figure has occurred in recent years.

In good part, the lowering of the nation's sights with respect to unemployment and inflation is simply an acceptance of what has occurred and a tribute to the stubbornness of the problems involved. It is a reflection, too, of the belief that the two goals are in conflict with one another and that some kind of compromise within the extremes is necessary. This is the dilemma embodied in the Phillips Curve which has recently become the center of sharp controversy among professional experts. The great majority of economists, however, would agree that, barring drastic institutional changes, a reduction of the unemployment rate to the 4 percent level would lead to a rapid rise in the price level; in fact, many economists hold the view that even bringing down the rate to 6 percent would result in an observable though not necessarily marked rise in the rate of inflation.[1]

The other side of the coin, whether lowering the annual rate of price increases to 4 percent or less would adversely affect the jobless rate, is less clear although, again, the majority of economists would lean toward the affirmative position. The basis for the latter view is that the restrictive fiscal and monetary policies which would be needed to achieve such a modest rate of price increase would choke off job expansion well below full employment, pushing up the unemployment rate to unacceptable levels. As a result, pressures to avoid the adverse consequences of unduly low rates of either unemployment or inflation have forced a compromise somewhere in the 4 to 6 percent "middle range" of target figures in the unemployment-inflation relationship.

Thus, the principal factor underlying the postwar uptrend in unemployment and the acceptance of higher unemployment goals over this period lies in the fact that the American economy, along with the other advanced industrial societies in the free world, has become increasingly inflation prone. The implication for policy generally derived from this fact is that the recurrence of severe inflationary episodes in the postwar period can largely be attributed to governmental efforts to achieve lower levels of unemployment. This latter proposition, while enjoying wide acceptance, is open to serious criticism as the later discussion shows.

The dominant issue, however, confronting macroeconomic policymaking in recent years is the emergence of stagflation: high inflation coupled with high unemployment. Instead of the either-or choice originally

---

1. See, for example, Lloyd G. Reynolds, *Labor Economics and Labor Relations,* 7th ed. (Englewood Cliffs, NJ: Prentice-Hall, 1978), p. 216.

posed by the Phillips Curve, the "new" curve points to adverse changes on both fronts and, as a consequence, a no-win position for policymakers. If, for example, consumer prices are rising at an annual rate above 6 percent and unemployment has also moved above this target figure, should monetary and fiscal policies be made primarily restrictive or expansive? If a decrease in the unemployment rate results from an expansionary demand policy, will this merely accentuate inflation and in the longer run force the unemployment rate back up again? If, on the other hand, inflation is slowed by a restrictive demand policy, will this simply push up the unemployment level still higher? In the context of the "new" Phillips Curve, can it even be argued that a fall in aggregate demand will in fact significantly reduce the pace of inflation? While clear-cut answers to these questions are certainly not to be expected, a discussion of some of the issues they raise is necessary to an understanding of the problem addressed in this study.

The Unemployment-Inflation Relationship Since World War II

The outstanding feature of business expansions in the period since World War II was the impact of war and its aftermath on the unemployment-inflation relationship. It was only in war-dominated environments that the unemployment rate fell below 4 percent. True, there were two peacetime expansions, one in 1954-57 when the rate fell to 4.1 percent by the fourth quarter of 1956, and another in 1961-65 when it fell to 4.5 percent by the fourth quarter of 1965, but the rate only declined into the 3 percent-and-less zone under war or war-related conditions. It is also worth noting that the wartime unemployment lows were closely geared to the relative domestic impact of the different conflicts: in World War II the unemployment rate fell to 1.2 percent in 1944, in the Korean War it fell to 2.9 percent in 1953, and in the Vietnam War it fell to 3.5 percent in 1969. While the view that genuine full employment can only be achieved in this country under wartime conditions is frequently criticized, the postwar record at least lends it prima facie credence.

The other side of this view, that major upsurges in prices are also a product of war, seems hardly less plausible. The financial excesses and economic strains associated with wars have had profound effects on prices, wages and costs which extend over long periods of time. The inflationary forces unleashed by the successive surges in wartime expenditures, and to a less extent by the continuing cold war outlays, gave a pronounced inflationary tilt to the economy during the postwar years. Between 1945 and 1972 there were four periods when the Consumer Price Index rose at a faster annual rate than 2 percent: 1945-48 (+11 percent), 1950-52 (+6 percent), 1956-58 (+3 percent), and 1965-72 (+5 percent). In terms of percentage point increases, as shown in Table 2-1, these four periods accounted for roughly 84 percent of the increase in consumer prices in the 1945-72 period, providing the major explanation of the inflation during these years.

Three of the four intervals were dominated by wartime or immediate postwar developments. If inflation as a serious problem is defined as a rise in prices in excess of 2 percent per year, it is clear that in the 1945-72 period it was almost wholly a war-related phenomenon, the one exception being the 1956-58 episode. It follows that the full employment achieved in the war periods was gained at the cost of serious price-wage instability later on. Over this twenty-five year period, on the other hand, the pursuit of full employment in peacetime environments did not generate serious inflationary pressures. Thus the onset of such pressures was due to the exegencies of wartime which in turn generated full employment or over full employment conditions. Aggregate demand in the latter sense needs to be viewed in quite a different light from aggregate demand which results from a full employment policy pursued in peacetime if for no other reason than that the positions and future outlooks of business, workers and the buying public are so different in the two environments.

Table 2-1
Percentage Point Increases in the Index of Consumer Prices for Selected Periods, 1945-1972

Selected periods	CPI indexes (1967 = 100)	Percentage point increases	Percentage share of 1945-1972 total increase*
1945-48	54 - 72	18	25
1950-52	72 - 80	8	11
1956-58	81 - 87	6	8
1966-72	97 - 125	28	39
Total point increase during selected periods	--	60	84
Total increase over entire 1945-72 period	54 - 125	71	--

*Differences in figures due to rounding.
Source: U.S. Department of Labor, Bureau of Labor Statistics.

The view, therefore, that demand management can no longer be used as the major weapon for bringing down the unemployment level in this country rests almost wholly on the experience of the relatively few years that have elapsed since 1972. Not surprisingly, scholars remain divided as to the weight that should be given various factors in explaining the emergence of stagflation, the persistence of severe inflation in the face of relatively high levels of unemployment, during this period. Two general explanations have received the most attention. The first holds that the federal government's fiscal and monetary policies have proven seriously unstabilizing, leading to excessive expansions as in 1972 and

1978 followed by contractions as in 1974 or slowdowns as in 1980. These cyclical distortions, it is argued, have fed into a longer-run type of imbalance in which workers, firms and other major groups come to expect a continued rise in prices and act accordingly, thereby building a rising inflation rate into the system even when market conditions have become quite negative. While the term full employment is often used rather loosely, the thrust of this line of argument is that the government's pursuit of this objective during these years and earlier has been the chief cause of the country's economic difficulties.

The other general approach stresses influences stemming from both long and short term changes that have occurred in supply and cost conditions. A number of investigators, notably the late R.A. Gordon and George Perry, uncovered convincing evidence that since the mid-1950s the composition of the nation's labor force has shifted towards a higher percentage of unemployment-prone groups: young and female workers, particularly the nonwhite members of these two groups. These investigators concluded that this shift alone would explain a rise of as much as a full percentage point in the minimum unemployment rate at which inflationary pressures on wages and prices would begin to mount. More recently, national attention has centered on the dramatic increase in energy prices which occurred in 1974 and again in 1979 as a result of actions by the OPEC countries. Poor harvests combined with rising world demand for food and other raw material supplies have also generated powerful inflationary forces in recent years. Additional upward pressures on unit costs have been felt in a number of industries because of the spread of environmental, health, safety and other types of regulations. As a result of these and related developments, costs have risen in a variety of fields, outlays for new equipment have slackened and the trend in labor productivity has become distinctly less favorable.

The two approaches entail radically different methods for dealing with persistent unemployment in the face of rapidly rising prices, the first emphasizing the need for throttling down the expansionary demand policies of government and the second, removing supply bottlenecks and cost-raising practices resulting from governmental action. Lacking any clear-cut basis for choosing one approach over the other, policymakers can be expected to move along both lines, with major stress on demand restraint as labor and product markets become increasingly tight and a cyclical peak in the economy emerges, or shifting major attention to cost-reducing measures if, as seems likely, long-run inflationary pressures become the dominant problem. Beyond this rather bland finding there are certain features of recent experience with respect to the persistence of unemployment in strong expansion periods that are worth noting.

First and most important, aggregate demand policy was sufficiently expansionary in the 1975-78 period to bring the unemployment rate down from 8.5 percent to 6 percent of the civilian labor force, with total civilian employment rising by nearly 10 million over the three-year period. When inflation accelerated in 1979, demand policy became increasingly restrictive but not so aggressively as to cause a rise, at least in the short run, in the unemployment level. Maintaining a relatively steady uptrend in aggregate demand after 1975 proved more effective in opening job opportunities for nonwhite males 20 years of age and older than any other demographic group, reducing their unemployment rate by three percentage points from 11.7 to 8.6 percent between 1975 and 1978. There was also a three percentage point drop during these years among nonwhite females in the 16-19 year age range, but among the other unemployment-prone groups, white and nonwhite females 20 years old and over, the drop in unemployment during this cyclical expansion period was disappointingly small. As in previous upswings, the vital role played by expansionary monetary and fiscal policies in bringing down both the overall jobless rate and the jobless rate among the structurally unemployed was clearly evident.

Second, as the workings of the Phillips Curve would predict, the same expansionary policies served to heighten the inflationary surge in prices that occurred between 1976 and 1979, but how much of the inflation should be attributed to the fiscal and monetary policies of the federal government as against external shocks to the economy remains a matter of controversy. The clearest instance of the important role of aggregate demand policy came in 1978 when the annual rate of increase in consumer prices other than for food and energy, the so-called basic inflation rate, jumped from 6.4 to 8.6 percent, a rise of some two percentage points over the previous year. Actually, both fiscal and monetary policies moved towards restraint during 1978 but it is generally agreed that the expansionary moves of the three preceding years had their major inflationary impact in the 1978-79 period. It was during this period that markets for certain major types of labor became quite tight and upward pressures on wages relative to productivity became more pronounced.

As the foregoing indicates, the hardest argument to answer against using demand expansion policies to push the unemployment rate below 6 percent, but also the vaguest, is that the impact of such policies can be long delayed and that their ultimate effects may prove to be cumulative in nature. This line of contention is sometimes broadened to suggest that, in the face of these policies, the attitudes of workers, employers and consumers towards inflation change and the entire wage, price and spending level increases as a result. Whatever the precise explanation, it is obvious that in view of recent experience, policymakers will have to give much more weight to longer-run effects of aggregate demand changes than previously thought.

Third, and this sharply modifies the point just noted, the inflation which took hold in this country in the course of the 1970s appeared to develop a life of its own quite unrelated to any short term countermoves in aggregate demand policy. Whether such countermoves would prove an effective, much less an efficient, way to reduce the inflation rate even in the longer-run is open to serious question. The weight of opinion among investigators is, in fact, it would not. Differences in emphasis abound, with some investigators stressing the importance of worker, employer and public expectations about the future course of prices while others stress the after effects on unit costs and per capita real incomes of past increases in prices. Nevertheless, there is general agreement that the inflation of the 1970s got built into the economy in a way that, short of severely restrictive fiscal and monetary policies maintained over several years, could perhaps be slowed but certainly not reversed by usual demand management. George Perry, for example, in his investigation of the problem, concluded that if unemployment were raised 1 percent above the 5.5 percent level and if there were no serious external shocks to the economy, it would take three years to reduce the inflation rate by one percentage point, and the extra point of unemployment would cost over a million jobs and some $60 billion in real output each year. He concluded:

> The evidence is that inflation would slow only gradually in response to holding back aggregate demand, and that the cost in lost employment and output per point of disinflation would be large.[2]

The economic and political difficulties besetting contractions in aggregate demand as a policy for bringing down the inflation rate are widely recognized, but precisely why this is so remains a matter of controversy. A key element in this

---

2. George L. Perry, *Slowing the Wage-Price Spiral: The Macroeconomic View,* Brookings Papers on Economic Activity, 2 (1978), pp. 285-286.

controversy is whether the American economy has entered a long term slowdown in investment, technological improvements and labor productivity, or whether the rise in the inflation rate is due to shorter term, ad hoc supply-cost influences such as shifts in the relative size of demographic groups or the price actions in 1973 and 1979 by OPEC. In any event, the record is clear that during most of the 1970s the basic inflation rate was on an upward trend that would have continued for a number of years even if aggregate demand policy had been considerably less expansionary. The upshot was that any additional inflationary influence attributable to demand policy expansion came on top of an already high basic inflationary rate, thereby pulling the overall rate up to an unacceptable level. This in turn led to increasing pressure to rein in any expansion in aggregate demand well before full employment, as usually defined, was attained. As a consequence, the sustained rise in aggregate demand that was needed to draw down the major categories of structural unemployment was effectively precluded.

Fourth, the previous analysis suggests that since a step-up in inflation on top of an already high basic rate of price increase can occur at almost any level of unemployment, the effort to identify some minimum noninflationary unemployment rate becomes largely beside the point. Despite repeated efforts to determine what this minimum figure is, compared to what it was, say, twenty years ago, the estimates remain too imprecise to serve as a guide to fiscal and monetary policies. The principal difficulty is that there is no way of determining the effect of shifts in labor force participation rates, the so-called "interaction" effect.[3]

---

3. According to a review of recent studies of the subject, the interaction effect accounts for as much as one-half of the total increase of about 1 percentage point that appears to have occurred in the 1976 vs. the 1956 unemployment rate. Joseph Antos, Wesley Mellon, and Jack E. Triplett, "What is a Current Equivalent to Unemployment Rates of the Past," *Monthly Labor Review,* March 1979, p. 39.

Even more important, in an environment like the 1970s, the pace of inflation may prove as unacceptably high when the unemployment level is 7 percent as when it is 5 percent. If the long term trend in inflation holds to 6 percent or more, almost any degree of aggregate demand stimulus will be seen as inducing serious inflationary pressures even if unemployment is running well above 6 percent. Supporters of this view will doubtless argue, and with considerable justification, that it is extremely difficult to determine when cost-push as opposed to demand-pull price pressures are the dominant factor in determining the pace of inflation. Given this uncertainty it would be only prudent to avoid any sharp upward moves in the fiscal and monetary aggregates even though labor and product markets remain relatively loose. Indeed it follows that policy should aim at decreasing the rate of increase in demand expansion before the point is reached where a cost-induced inflation becomes converted into a cost-and-demand one.

The case for beginning to taper demand expansion relatively early on in cyclical upswings also rests on the fact noted earlier that the effects of restrictive demand policies are often long-delayed and, more particularly, if the restrictions are both too late and too sweeping, the economy can be forced into a severe recession. Contrariwise, if total demand rises slowly and begins to taper early, the necessity for a sharp cutback later becomes less likely.

This approach to demand policy, of course, has to be applied somewhat flexibly, depending on the type of cyclical expansion involved and on the longer term prospects for the economy. In line with traditional macroeconomic analysis, the closer the economy approaches its full employment potential, the stronger the case becomes for slowing the pace of demand expansion. Reliable estimates of the economy's short term potential at any given moment of time are admittedly hazardous, whether expressed in terms of the minimum inflation level of unemployment or the gap between actual and potential production. At the same time, the implication for demand management of a given jump in the annual rate of inflation certainly differs if the unemployment level is in the 6-7 percent as opposed to the 4-5 percent range.

The other side of this approach to policymaking, however, is no less important: demand expansion, while slowing, would need to continue at a sufficiently high rate to prevent any significant rise in the general unemployment level and, even more, to induce a significant reduction in joblessness among the structurally unemployed. If demand in later phases of an expansion is not maintained close to rates prevailing in earlier phases, effective action to reach the hard-to-employ is likely to prove abortive, since their job status largely depends on the length and strength of a particular expansion. This could mean using demand stimulus to push the overall unemployment rate as low as 5 or even 4 percent, a policy that would only be defensible if employed under special circumstances and with a great deal of care. The fact that there is no clearly defined noninflationary minimum level of unemployment adds considerably to the flexibility of aggregate demand policy but certainly does not lessen the need for restraint in such policy as low levels of unemployment are approached. As developed in later chapters, this is clearly not a sufficient condition for dealing with the problem of structural unemployment, but it is a necessary one. It underscores, too, the point noted earlier that a given rate of inflation calls for very different demand management policies if labor markets become extremely tight from those called for if they remain relatively loose.

Conclusion

In recent years there has been increasing acceptance of the view that government demand management has proven singularly ineffective as a means for reducing unemployment without causing serious inflation. This view rests on a series of assumptions which, to varying degrees, remain largely unproven.

First, it assumes that any significant rise in the rate of inflation is attributable to an increase in the level of aggregate demand. Careful investigations of inflations, especially those of recent origin, do not support this simple type of explanation. Increasing weight, instead, is being given to developments on the supply side such as adverse cost trends and external shocks to the economy. While aggregate demand is still given a prominent role, exclusive attention to this aspect of the inflationary process is now considered quite misleading.

Second, it assumes that the *continuation* of an inflationary process, quite aside from its sources of origin, is the result of an increase in aggregate demand. Recent investigators, however, have shifted the focus of attention to certain long term influences such as trends in labor productivity and the emergence of institutional arrangements with respect to wage-setting which have given inflationary developments a life of their own. Again, this serves to break any close link between upward or downward shifts in aggregate demand and the underlying, largely predetermined rate of inflation. To this extent, expansionary aggregate demand policy can be given a broader, not a narrower, role in bringing down the unemployment rate.

Third, this view assumes that any significant rise in the inflation rate has been caused by overstimulative fiscal or monetary actions of the federal government. Even if aggregative demand changes are seen as controlling in this regard, it does not follow that such changes are solely or even primarily the result of federal countercyclical demand policies. Other sources of demand influence may be no less involved, among them budgetary actions on the part of state and local governments, policy moves of private lending institutions, business decisions with respect to inventory accumulations and capital projects, household spending decisions and shifts in international financial relationships. Whether a particular change in federal fiscal and/or monetary policies should be viewed as the crucial variable among all the welter of determinants, both public and private, bearing on the level of aggregate demand calls for careful appraisal of any given situation or period. Unless it is argued that the federal government, in failing to take sufficient corrective action, is responsible for every marked increase in the inflation rate, whatever its source, a much more guarded explanation is indicated.

Fourth, this view assumes that in undertaking an expansionary demand policy, the federal government's only goal is to achieve full employment. While the rhetoric surrounding some fiscal and monetary moves lends a certain plausibility to this interpretation, other purposes such as a stronger defense posture, aid to farmers, slum clearance, an improved highway system and protection of small business are in the aggregate likely to be of equal or greater importance. The fact that a full employment *condition,* induced by expansionary moves to achieve purposes of the latter sort, may have serious inflationary consequences needs to be clearly distinguished from a full employment *policy* in which none of these purposes is necessarily involved. Seen in this light, the effort to achieve full employment has been widely criticized on grounds that are not actually deserved.

The conclusion emerging from this discussion is that aggregate demand policy, if implemented along lines outlined earlier, can reduce the unemployment level to at least the 5 -5.5 percent range without inducing serious inflationary consequences. While not markedly less than the usual estimates made by others, the difference is large enough to have important implications for policies aimed at the problem of prosperity unemployment. The reasons for this conclusion will be made clear in succeeding chapters.

Chapter 3
Reducing Frictional and Seasonal Unemployment

Unemployment not attributable to a general deficiency in demand can be divided into structural and frictional types of joblessness. Chief attention in terms of policy has quite appropriately centered on the structural elements of unemployment, but the frictional elements also deserve consideration in any analysis of the prosperity unemployment problem.

Even under a condition of full employment in which total job openings equal total job seekers, some unemployment will exist because the matching of job openings and job seekers is not instantaneous. The time it takes for an employer and a job applicant to find each other and agree on terms entails temporary periods of joblessness which at any one time will affect millions of workers, perhaps as many as 2 or 2.5 percent of the country's labor force. The total size of this group of workers apparently does not vary much over the cycle, but its composition and character changes sharply as the economy moves from low to high levels of activity.

It is generally accepted that labor markets in this country do a relatively poor job of matching job seekers and job suppliers. In a number of other countries, notably England, Germany and Sweden, the process of allocating workers to available job openings is handled with considerably more efficiency than here. These countries are much smaller than the

United States, their economies less diverse, their populations more homogeneous, and the role of government considerably more important. Whether because of these or other factors, workers and employers in these countries are much readier to rely on public administered labor exchanges to fill new jobs than in the United States.

Particularly in the case of Sweden, a quite comprehensive set of policies has emerged over the past thirty years to assist unemployed or underemployed workers find openings, secure mobility grants, and thus iron out employment between areas and industries. These selective measures are often addressed to both structural and aggregate demand types of unemployment, but their main purpose is to reduce frictional unemployment.[1]

In the 1960s, turnover rates in manufacturing (total separations per 100 employees) ran 70 percent to 100 percent higher in this country than in West Germany, Great Britain or Italy. In the boom year of 1973, employment in the United States averaged 84 million persons per month, but about 100 million persons worked at some time during the year. During the same year, unemployment averaged 4 million persons per month, but more than three times this number experienced some unemployment in the year.[2] While an inescapable feature of changes in methods of production, in the needs and preferences of both workers and employers, and in the search times involved in reconciling their preferences, this extremely high movement into and out of jobs and into and out of the labor force seems both economically and socially wasteful. Indeed, if the average job search-recruiting period could be cut from four weeks to

---

1. For an illuminating account of Swedish experience in this regard, see the essay by Rudolf Meidner and Rolf Andersson in *Manpower Programs in the Policy Mix,* Lloyd Ulman, ed. (Baltimore: Johns Hopkins University Press, 1973), Ch. 5.

2. *Economic Report of the President, 1975,* pp. 88 and 101.

two weeks through improved matching procedures, the amount of frictional unemployment would be cut in half.

The case for action along these lines is especially strong in periods of prosperity when the role of demand deficiency as a determinant of unemployment lessens, and the relative importance of the frictional component in whatever unemployment still obtains necessarily increases. George Perry has estimated that, at a national unemployment rate of 6 percent, a prime age male (twenty-five to thirty-four) would take an average of 6.6 weeks to find a new job, but an average of only 4.3 weeks if the national unemployment rate were 3 percent.[3] Since there is little prospect of the national unemployment rate even approaching the latter figure in peacetime, careful consideration should be given to adopting measures deliberately aimed at improving the job search-worker recruiting process at higher rates of unemployment.

Characteristics of Frictional Unemployment

As the foregoing suggests, the nature of frictional unemployment changes as the national unemployment rate varies. At the 2-3 percent level, vacancies approach or even exceed the number of job applicants at prevailing wage rates. In a dynamic economy where job seeking and worker recruitment are largely a matter of individual choice, imbalances in labor markets will still obtain even in these highly favorable circumstances, but most such imbalances will be temporary and limited. Even if particular workers are involuntarily displaced, with a modicum of search effort they will be able to find comparably attractive openings; so it is largely a matter of personal preference which of a variety of openings they choose. Employers, on the other hand, will face

---

3. George L. Perry, *Unemployment Flows in the U.S. Labor Market,* Brookings Papers on Economic Activity, 2 (1972) cited in Reynolds, *Labor Economics and Labor Relations,* p. 128.

somewhat longer search times than in periods of looser markets and may have to lower hiring standards accordingly. The imbalances occurring under these conditions constitute frictional unemployment in its pure form, and, so far as public policy is concerned, can be largely left to the determination of market influences.

Especially in prosperities, much of the mobility is essential, in both a short-run and long-run sense, to the economy's effective performance. One of the striking features of the long expansion of the 1960s was the fact that the voluntary quit rate in manufacturing rose from 1.3 per 100 employees in 1960 to 2.7 in 1969 while the layoff rate fell from 2.4 to 1.2 over the same period; in the recessionary years after 1969 the opposite pattern developed.[4] The limited data available indicate that rates of voluntary quits do not become very high even in prosperities, but to the extent inter-job movements are genuinely voluntary, they play a crucially important role in the economy.

As unemployment rates rise above this minimum level, imbalances are not ironed out so quickly. As soon as the jobless rate begins to move up and labor markets loosen, interferences begin to appear in the matching process. The resulting unemployment can still be appropriately classified as frictional as long as the number of vacancies and job applicants remain, on an overall basis, roughly equal, but the matching task now becomes subject to a variety of temporary and minor impediments. The need arises for fuller and more extensive information on job openings, for longer commuting trips to places of employment, and for rather different combinations of skills on the part of job ap-

---

4. U.S. Department of Labor, *Employment and Earnings,* Vol. 11 (June 1965), Table D-1, p. 55, and Vol. 22 (May 1976, Table D-1, p. 109, cited in Gordon F. Bloom and Herbert R. Northrup, *Economics of Labor Relations,* 8th ed., (Homewood, IL: Richard D. Irwin, 1977), p. 243.

plicants. It is not possible to determine exactly when such interferences no longer are frictional and become structural in nature, but as long as they are readily removable they can still be treated as falling in the former category.

A chief factor explaining why it is so difficult to bring down the frictional unemployment rate relates to the nature of the search-recruitment process itself. Job matching in labor markets is often a complicated, highly personalized procedure affected by a variety of conditions, requirements, prospects and individual worker-employer preferences. This is reflected in the diverse, often individualized, ways employers and job seekers "find" each other. A survey of 20 middle-sized cities during the last six months of 1974 found that 80 percent of all job finders applied directly to employers, while 70 percent spoke to friends and relatives and 60 percent consulted with business associates. The Employment Service, on the other hand, was consulted by only 28 percent of all job finders.[5] The very variety of methods characteristic of labor markets in this country would make it extremely difficult to achieve much more orderly patterns of job search even under the most prosperous conditions.

A principal theme of recent investigations of frictional unemployment is that this type of unemployment is marked by a continually changing composition of workers who either have recently been employed or have just come into the labor force. The flow of workers into and out of employment of this nature gives rise to, and is the product of, a two-sided search process which incurs important costs for both the job seeker and the hiring firm but which provides important mutual benefits as well. The principal question facing

---

5. U.S. Department of Labor, *Recruitment, Job Search, and the United States Employment Service,* R & D Monograph 43 (1976), pp. 1-57. A job finder typically used more than one method of search.

the job seeker is whether the gain that may derive from a longer and wider search will more than outweigh the lost earnings, travel expenses and other costs involved. Similar considerations having to do with costs of recruitment, screening and placement versus the expected productive value of the individual who is finally hired apply to the employer's search.

Viewed in this light, unemployment of a frictional nature is a valuable, indeed necessary, component of labor market activity. Since, according to this view, a major part of the unemployment experienced in periods of prosperity is of this nature, the concern of public policymakers in such periods should, it is argued, be limited to making the search process as effective and efficient as the added costs entailed would justify: more complete data on job opportunities and job applicants; readily accessible facilities for bringing "buyers and sellers" together; and fuller information on other possible openings and applicants as well as on less immediate considerations such as commuting costs, industry prospects and labor supply trends.

It follows from this view, too, that most unemployment in periods of prosperity is a matter of personal choice on the part of the workers and employers involved: job applicants who cannot find suitable work in an acceptably short time will either have to cut back their asking wage or remain out of work; employers who cannot find suitable workers in an acceptably short time will either have to raise their wage offers or not secure the additional workers they desire. Since job vacancies tend to rise in prosperous periods relative to unemployed workers and job applicants, it follows that the search process will on average entail less time in such periods than when business conditions are generally slack.

While providing important insights into labor market behavior and the nature of unemployment, this view has led to few if any useful recommendations for public policymakers. In the first place, the data reveal a marked difference between workers with limited skill, education and job experience as against those with more of these attributes. For the former, a pattern of frequent job changes, punctuated by periods of unemployment or withdrawal from the labor force, is much more typical than for the latter. In his study of the relatively prosperous 1972 economy when unemployment averaged only 5 percent, George Perry found that teenagers of either sex experienced an average of nearly two jobless spells a year as against men over 45 who had an average of only one spell every four to five years. Between these two extremes the frequency of unemployment spells declined steadily as the age of workers of either sex increased, but the average duration of such spells varied in the opposite direction.[6]

It could be argued that a worker experiencing such frequent spells of joblessness is following a perfectly rational procedure: sampling different jobs until the best available opening is found, a condition that is most likely to obtain when business activity is at a high level. This doubtless applies to considerable numbers of teenagers. A roughly similar line of argument appears to hold good for employed women since they move into and out of the labor force more frequently than men and labor force entry and re-entry involves a high probability of becoming unemployed.[7]

On the other hand, such rapid movements into and out of unemployment may well be involuntary in the sense that the workers are subject to insurmountable barriers which limit them to some one, low-level type of work. In such instances,

---

6. Perry, *Unemployment Flows in the Labor Market,* p. 260.

7. S.T. Marston, *Employment Instability and High Unemployment Rates,* Brookings Papers on Economic Activity, 1 (1976), pp. 170-178. His data cover the relatively prosperous years from 1967 to 1973.

job turnover entails little or no cost either to the workers or employers involved since in market terms the jobs, work environments and workers themselves tend to be almost completely homogeneous at the very lowest skill levels. Abnormally high rates of job turnover of this sort, therefore, are likely to reflect structural limitations surrounding the job search process rather than frictional elements as normally defined.

Quite aside from these considerations, serious question has recently been raised about the importance of frictional unemployment in relation to total unemployment. Earlier investigations had suggested that much of the latter consisted of persons suffering relatively frequent but brief spells of joblessness. A recent study by Kim B. Clark and Lawrence H. Summers, however, revealed that in 1974, when the overall unemployment rate was relatively low, only 36 percent of unemployment was attributable to persons finding a job within three months. Indeed, when account is taken of movements into and out of the labor force, these investigators concluded that the average person unemployed at a point in time in this kind of economic environment will experience almost six months of joblessness during a year. Finally, they concluded that, rather than being widely dispersed among the population, unemployment is highly concentrated, with over half of all joblessness traceable to persons out of work for more than six months in a year. Thus, the concentration of joblessness is far greater than would be expected from normal turnover; according to the Clark-Summers study, the latter "accounts for at most 1.5 points or about 25 percent of unemployment at high employment levels."[8] Based on a detailed review of the evidence, they concluded that if the counting of the unemployed were

---

8. Kim B. Clark and Lawrence H. Summers, *Labor Market Dynamics and Unemployment: A Reconsideration,* Brookings Papers on Economic Activity, 1 (1979), pp. 16-17. The term "high employment" refers to an unemployment rate of 6 percent.

limited to all those persons with less than five weeks of unemployment during the year, the measured unemployment rate would fall only from 6 percent to 5.75 percent, but if the counting were limited to those with six months or more unemployment, the jobless rate would fall from 6 percent to 3.5 percent.[9]

This finding is admittedly somewhat altered, however, when the evidence is put into a cyclical as opposed to a noncyclical context. Thus, in 1969 when the overall unemployment rate was only 3.5 percent, unemployment per person averaged a little over 12 weeks per unemployed person as against nearly 19 weeks in 1975 when overall unemployment was 8.5 percent. Similarly, the proportion of the labor force unemployed for only one to four weeks stood at approximately 3.5 percent in both 1969 and 1975 but the proportion unemployed 15 weeks or more came to only 2 percent in 1969 as against 9.1 percent in 1975. Not surprisingly, the data for 1974, when unemployment was 5.6 percent, fell roughly midway between the 1969 and 1975 patterns.[10]

Much of the controversy over the distinction between voluntary, short term and involuntary, long term unemployment turns on where the minimum non-inflationary rate of unemployment proves to be; if the minimum level, for example, turns out to be as low as 5 percent, the part played by voluntary unemployment resulting from interjob movement would account for a much larger proportion of total unemployment than if the level turns out to be as high as 6 percent. As indicated in the preceding chapter, the relative importance of voluntary unemployment in the frictional, job search sense, as opposed to involuntary unemployment due to limited aggregate demand and/or structural barriers, can

---

9. Ibid., p. 72.

10. Ibid., Table 4, p. 36.

be significantly affected by small changes in the non-inflationary minimum unemployment level.

Since it is highly probable that the minimum sustainable unemployment rate will remain above 5 percent for the foreseeable future, it follows that public policy should primarily be aimed at reducing the barriers which result in involuntary unemployment among particular demographic groups. This does not mean that efforts to improve the short term allocation performance of labor markets should not continue but that the major thrust of policy should be directed towards the elimination of more permanent and fundamental barriers to employment over which severely disadvantaged job seekers have no control.

Regarding the latter objective, the characteristics of an efficiently functioning system of labor markets—open access to job opportunities, active bidding by both buyers and sellers, shifts in demand and supplies in response to changes in market conditions and the other features of a fully competitive environment—provide a sound framework for public policymaking. Indeed, the principal guide to such policy might well be to make it possible for those members of disadvantaged groups who are now largely excluded from most of the established labor markets to become active participants in them. The salient feature of such markets, especially in periods of general prosperity, is a widening of opportunities for upward mobility on the part of workers, whether employed, unemployed or outside the labor force, who have the qualifications, incentive and initiative to take advantage of them. In periods of sluggish business when applicants are running ahead of vacancies, programs designed to help workers meet these requirements are likely to face almost insurmountable difficulties; it is in periods of sustained expansion, as already indicated, that such programs have the greatest chance of success and should be pressed most vigorously. While higher skill levels would be involved, principal attention would need to center in these circumstances on helping workers overcome barriers to first-level, relatively unskilled jobs which are likely to lead to stable, long term careers.

Policy measures aimed at promoting the upward, or indeed lateral, mobility of disadvantaged groups would need to be closely integrated with general programs designed to promote the more efficient allocation of labor, on the one hand, and specific programs to help disadvantaged workers overcome structural barriers to employment on the other. This twofold aspect of the work of the Employment Service and other agencies seeking to improve the performance of labor markets is examined in the next section of this report.

Role of the Employment Service

Most discussions of efforts to improve job allocation procedures in this country center on the limitations of the federal-state Employment Service (ES) and how it might be strengthened. Many of the problems besetting the Service can be traced to the fact that, while funding is provided by the federal government, day to day administration rests with the states—subject only to general federal guidelines.

Historical reviews of ES emphasize that, since its establishment in 1933, it has been subjected to a bewildering series of policy mandates ranging from helping employers find qualified workers, to providing manpower information and services to a broad spectrum of workers, to providing a still wider range of services to the lowest qualified category of workers. These changing goals have been superimposed on its responsibility, established in the 1930s, to administer the work test for unemployment insurance claimants. Given these changing, and to a considerable extent overlapping, mandates it would be surprising if it could be shown that ES has had any observable effect on the level of unemployment, the one policy goal under consideration here. There are certain functions of ES, however, which clearly bear on this goal, especially in periods of prosperity, so the question of whether these functions might be strengthened deserves attention.

The relevant ES activities are (1) providing workers and employers with basic current information on job openings and job applicants, (2) assisting workers in choosing careers and implementing career plans, (3) referring workers to job and training opportunities in the public sector pursuant to the WIN welfare and other government programs, (4) serving as a link between schools and other community institutions on the one hand, and job and training opportunities on the other. Besides the obvious difficulty that in many states and localities ES has not been given adequate funds and personnel to carry out these and other responsibilities effectively, are there other steps that could be taken to make ES more effective in lessening frictional unemployment?

The central problem facing ES is that it has not been able to win wide acceptance among company recruiters and job applicants, a result that can be attributed chiefly to the fact that it has become so closely identified with the handling of unemployment insurance claims and with the placement of unemployed, lower skilled workers in entry-level jobs. Ironically, by concentrating so much of its attention on unemployed and unemployment-prone workers, ES has tended to undercut its capacity to deal effectively with the more general jobless problem. Under present circumstances, recruiters looking for applicants for higher level jobs largely rely on other avenues of search. Especially in periods of prosperity, the rate of decrease in unemployment largely depends on how rapidly and how extensively job vacancies at these better levels are filled. As noted earlier, the effectiveness of public policy in reducing frictional unemployment under these circumstances largely depends on whether upward mobility can be extended to workers hitherto excluded from entering stable, career-related jobs. If the ES is to play an effective role in dealing with the kind of unemploy ment that persists into expansions, it will need to focus increased attention on this aspect of labor market activity.

Recent developments give little grounds for optimism on this score. The rapid rise in ES job placements from under 2 million in fiscal year 1971 to over 3 million in fiscal 1974 was interrupted in the 1974-75 recession, resuming, but at an apparently lower rate, during the subsequent expansion. In upswing periods, as noted in the 1977 *Employment and Training Report,* "ES job applicants are more likely to be young, inexperienced, economically disadvantaged, or older workers—categories that are hard to place."[11] Under the Comprehensive Employment and Training Act (CETA), passed in December 1973, chief responsibility for administering training and related services was delegated to local and state governments. Not surprisingly, the latter are relying extensively on the ES offices to secure jobs for disadvantaged workers. Specifically, this has meant that ES is heavily involved in referring workers under various recently authorized public employment programs, the same role it was earlier assigned under the WIN program. The work requirement emphasis in the recently proposed welfare reform legislation, if enacted, will have a similar impact on the activity of ES. Important as these responsibilities are, they clearly do not lead to greater ES acceptance by recruiters and applicants concerned with better quality jobs and personnel.

The conflict between the needs of the lowest and highest (or lower and higher) qualified job applicants will probably never be wholly resolved for the ES, at least given its present

---

11. *Employment and Training Report of the President, 1977* (Washington: Government Printing Office, 1978), p. 75.

limited resources. If it is required to assume both roles, as now seems likely, every effort should be made by ES to distinguish applicants at all levels—the least as well as the most experienced and/or qualified—and to handle referrals accordingly. Employment Service offices try to do this now, even with respect to applicants within the least-skilled category, but few if any have the staff resources to carry out this function effectively. If it is assigned still broader responsibilities with respect to the lowest skilled category of job seekers without corresponding additions to its resources, general acceptance of the ES by employers and higher skilled workers will inevitably lessen still more.

Job Banks

The principal approach adopted by ES for dealing with this dilemma is to develop computerized job bank systems in major localities, an effort that was launched in Baltimore in 1968. Under these systems, job orders submitted to ES are accumulated daily and published in a job-bank book the next day, thus making information on reported openings currently available on a wide basis. In the early 1970s steps were taken to develop a nationwide job-bank network and, what is much more ambitious, to establish computerized job matching systems which would match up the characteristics of workers and the requirements of jobs; implementation of the latter program, however, has thus far been confined to only a few states.

By computerizing job information in this way, ES hopes most job seekers will be able to find suitable openings on their own, permitting its staff to concentrate more attention on difficult individual cases. The danger is that, instead of insuring that employers will find better qualified applicants coming from ES as a result of this systems approach, they will find just the opposite. Much of course depends on how far ES can go in developing adequate counseling and other individualized methods for dealing with the needs of different job seekers. In good part, the outcome will depend on whether ES can develop tighter evaluation criteria for making referrals or whether it continues to place major emphasis on sheer numbers of placements.

Even if ES achieves marked progress along these lines in matching up job seekers and company recruiters, the barriers to steady employment confronting many disadvantaged workers would remain largely untouched. To get at this underlying issue more far-reaching measures than merely facilitating the employment matching process will be needed, measures which ES is generally precluded from undertaking. There is one crucial function in this connection, however, which is largely disregarded and which ES is in a better position to perform than any other agency: identifying unemployed and otherwise severely disadvantaged workers in need of individual counseling and personalized support who should be referred to special training or other types of programs and whose subsequent progress should be followed on a continuing basis. Responsibility for this coordinating-referral-follow up function is loosely handled or overlooked altogether under present circumstances. ES has taken limited steps in this direction in some localities; in other instances, other agencies have made a few efforts in this direction. Broadly speaking, however, this vitally important function has received little attention.

An individualized program of this sort would necessarily be limited to a relatively small number of workers. At first at least, careful procedures would be needed to determine who should be admitted to this special program, how relationships with cooperating agencies could best be implemented, and what methods of evaluation should be applied. The focus would presumably be on those workers, mostly young, inexperienced or with a modicum of skills, who are most likely to be lost sight of as they move between home, school, training center or other public agency, and temporary or permanent jobs. Because of the formidable difficulties confronting any program of this sort, strict limits would have to be set on the number of participants, particularly since its main objective would be to help disadvantaged workers secure not just any type of employment but rather jobs with definite career potential.

Commuting and Relocation Subsidies

One of the proposals that is frequently suggested for reducing frictional unemployment is to make it possible for displaced or other unemployed workers to commute greater distances or relocate in other communities where job openings are available. This is an important feature of employment policies in a number of European countries, most notably Sweden. Little, however, has been done along these lines in the United States.

Insofar as local commuting systems are concerned, the reason for this lack of attention is apparent. Adequate commuting facilities for jobless workers is but one aspect of a given community's transportation needs. It would be a most unusual circumstance where a major addition or change in a local transportation system could be justified on the needs of such workers alone. Special situations of this sort might well be allowed for, nonetheless. A community which could demonstrate that changes in its transportation facilities would significantly broaden job opportunities for an important group of disadvantaged workers should be able to apply for special federal funding; similar provision could be made for special situations where commuting fares would be subsidized in the interest of broader access to particular job markets. Such efforts, however, could only be undertaken on an individual, locality-by-locality basis.

A more practical approach, which has only been tried on a limited basis in this country, is to help jobless or underemployed workers through job information, resettlement assistance, and training find positions in other localities. Such efforts as have been made along these lines, unfortunately, have proven rather disappointing. The initial emphasis in the 1960s was on bringing new capital and services to high unemployment areas; thus, the focus of the Public Works and Economic Development Act of 1965 was on extending public works grants (highways, schools, health facilities and the like) to low-income communities and on giving employers financial inducements to move into such depressed areas. Effective implementation of this program was undercut by several factors, the chief one being that pressures to spread available funds widely in order to include localities other than low-income areas proved too strong.

Because of the difficulties encountered, the focus soon shifted to providing job opportunities in nearby growth centers and helping stranded workers find jobs in such centers through job information, resettlement assistance, and training. As matters turned out, funds available to the Economic Development Administration were far from adequate in many areas; most of the cities selected were below 200,000 in population, the minimum considered necessary for self-sustaining growth; other nearby cities which showed more growth potential had to be excluded; and funds expended on brick and mortar could probably have been better devoted to training, health care and the like.[12] Admittedly, experience has been largely limited to relocation efforts in rural localities, most notably some 60 pilot mobility assistance projects authorized by the Manpower Develop-

---

12. Niles Hansen, "Growth Centers, Human Resources and Rural Development" (University of Texas, Rural Labor Market Strategies Project, 1971), cited in Sar A. Levitan, Garth L. Mangum, and Ray Marshall, *Human Resources and Labor Markets* (New York: Harper and Row, 1972), p. 538.

ment and Training Act between 1965 and 1969 to help relocate more than 14,000 unemployed or underemployed workers and their families, chiefly from depressed rural areas and small towns.

Despite two recommendations to the contrary by the Department of Labor, Congress did not appropriate any separate funds for these projects after 1969, but several were carried forward with regular MDTA experimental and demonstration funds. The main aim of the projects was to help jobless, chiefly disadvantaged, workers in labor surplus areas overcome geographical distance barriers in finding work in strong job markets. The cost averaged about $800 per family, including about $300 for moving and settling in. While no systematic cost-benefit analysis has been undertaken, the cost level appears to be "relatively low compared with the possible cost to society of maintaining people in an unproductive situation."[13]

If relocation assistance grants were to be made widely available, a number of serious hurdles would have to be overcome. Care would have to be taken that jobs are available in the destination locations that would be in line with the abilities and needs of the relocatees. Workers recruited for the program should not be at such high skill and experience levels that relocation aid would be unnecessary nor at such low levels that the aid could not possibly lead to permanent moves. Provision would have to be made for a variety of supportive services, especially in the case of severely disadvantaged workers, including help in obtaining housing, arranging for transportation to worksites, securing health care and accommodating to wholly new community environments. Close links would have to be worked out between the implementing organizations (presumably the Employment Service offices) at both ends of the moves and

13. *Manpower Report of the President, 1971*, p. 137.

among the relevant manpower and community service bodies at the receiving end. The active cooperation of the hiring firms would of course be essential.[14] Any serious effort to use relocation grants as an important means for dealing with hard core unemployment in inner cities, as opposed to rural areas, would face even more formidable difficulties.

Despite the limited success of previous efforts in this direction and the complications besetting them, a resumption of a program of mobility aids deserves serious consideration. Carefully drawn criteria, plus continuous and careful monitoring along the lines indicated above would be essential. This approach, being highly selective, could not be expected to effect any marked improvement in job matching processes in labor markets generally. Its importance would increase, however, as job vacancies rose and instances of labor market supply tightness multiplied. While a program of mobility grants could probably never be a major answer to prosperity unemployment, it deserves a place in any serious attack on the problem.

The Carter Administration recently proposed a return to the approach undertaken in the early 1960s under which federal aid would be made available to localities in the format of investment tax credits and business credit supports, but this time the distribution of the funds would be limited to "distressed communities" or pockets within such communities alone. It is estimated that only about a third of the nation's communities would be eligible for help under this proposal but this would include most of the country's largest cities. That Congress will go along with the effort to limit the program in this way seems doubtful.[15]

---

14. Ibid., p. 138; see also Levitan, Mangum, and Marshall, *Human Resources and Labor Markets,* pp. 539-547.

15. *New York Times,* May 25, 1978.

Seasonal Unemployment

A number of important industries are subject to seasonal fluctuations in employment due to intrayear shifts in either supply or demand. The annual rise and fall in the teenage population entering and leaving the labor force with the closing and opening of schools is the principal seasonal influence operating on the side of labor supply. Changes in climatic conditions account for most of the seasonal instability in agriculture and construction. Other industries such as automobiles and clothing are affected by seasonal changes in demand which in turn result from custom, habit or style factors. While there is some indication that the seasonal element in unemployment in a number of industries has lessened somewhat since World War II, it still accounts for an important segment of the nation's jobless. Indeed, because of the seasonal supply pattern of young job seekers, the overall importance of seasonal unemployment has probably increased since World War II.

Calculations of the seasonal factor in unemployment are necessarily rough. With respect to the peak prosperity year of 1969, R.A. Gordon has estimated that seasonal joblessness accounted for about one-fifth of the nation's total unemployment or about 0.7 of that year's overall rate of 3.5 percent.[16] Using data on layoffs in manufacturing between 1958 and 1969, the only sector for which data are available, Daniel Hamermesh found that the seasonal factor accounted for about 31 percent of the total variation in layoffs or roughly .62 percentage points of an unemployment rate of 4 percent.[17] When the national unemployment

---

16. Lloyd Ulman, ed., *Manpower Programs in the Policy Mix,* essay by R.A. Gordon, p. 25. The estimate was based on a method previously developed by the Bureau of Labor Statistics.

17. Daniel S. Hamermesh, *Jobless Pay and the Economy* (Baltimore: Johns Hopkins University Press, 1977), p. 71.

rate is higher, the relative importance of seasonal unemployment would be less, although the absolute amount of seasonal joblessness would be somewhat greater than these estimates would indicate.

Any private or public effort to reduce seasonal unemployment would have to come to grips with the fact that the sources of this type of employment instability are diverse and are the by-product of long-standing conditions and practices. The seasonality factor in major branches of retail trade, automobile manufacture, clothing and the like have become imbedded in traditional patterns of the production and distribution system. Hiring practices in the longshoring industry based on the daily shape-up and reliance on casual labor, for example, contributed to the high degree of seasonability of employment in this field; it took many years of union pressure before recruitment was decasualized and employment in longshoring became stable. The problems besetting such stabilizing efforts are well illustrated in construction, a field long plagued by seasonal unemployment.

While weather conditions are the principal element bearing on the seasonality of construction employment and unemployment, other influences such as annual "moving days" and the presence of many small, weak firms incapable of using advanced building methods, are also important. The custom of fixed leasing dates and the practice of letting contracts in the spring have also been cited in this connection.[18] The technology and administrative skills are available to reduce seasonality in employment in the industry, as World War II experience made clear, but short of extreme shortage conditions, the higher costs of winter operations and the like pose serious barriers to improvement. In a careful study of

---

18. William Haber and Harold M. Levinson, *Labor Relations and Productivity in the Building Trades* (Ann Arbor, MI: Bureau of Industrial Relations, University of Michigan, 1956), Ch. 4.

the industry, Daniel Mills emphasized the importance of job opportunities for construction workers in other industries during the winter months, as well as in the construction industry itself; he concluded that reductions in seasonality occur when construction demand is high and labor supply conditions generally are tight, a largely unintended outcome resulting from peak season shortages and delays.[19]

Any serious effort to reduce seasonality in construction by increasing the level of work done in winter months would require changes in collective bargaining agreements, contractor practices and architects' specifications, as well as in contract enforcement activities on the part of the unions and, in the case of public works, on the part of the government. Mills argues that the most promising approach is for public owners to require, except in unusual cases, that work proceed through the winter months and to adopt appropriate specifications for temporary heating, lighting, and enclosure. A similar effort, after being reconciled with collective bargaining agreements, could be made in the private sector so that the requirements and specifications for winter work would be included in bid documents.[20]

The example of construction makes clear why attempts to reduce seasonal unemployment have yielded such meager results. While an aspect of frictional unemployment, the sources of seasonal joblessness differ from industry to industry and any serious effort to limit this type of unemployment would require collaborative effort by the particular employers, unions and public bodies involved. No overall national program which attempted to cover all major industries would seem feasible. Where conditions in particular industries give promise of success, efforts to reduce seasonal

---

19. Daniel O. Mills, *Industrial Relations and Manpower in Construction* (Cambridge, MA: MIT Press, 1972), p. 129.

20. Ibid., pp. 129-132.

unemployment would of course deserve public support, but it would not be appropriate to make such efforts a major focus of policy action with respect to the problem of persistent unemployment.

Conclusion

With certain reservations, the policy conclusion reached about seasonal unemployment can be applied to frictional unemployment generally. In part, this is due to the highly individualized and varied nature of this type of unemployment; in part, to the voluntary, "bettering myself" element that is frequently involved; in part to the influence of deepseated characteristics of labor markets which frequently lie behind the more pathological patterns of frictional unemployment.

This is not to deny that certain measures could be taken to improve the matching process in job markets in this country, measures such as stronger support for the Employment Service, more detailed, individualized information on job openings and job applicants, better counseling and coordination of efforts to help disadvantaged workers quality for career-oriented jobs, and expansion of programs to provide mobility assistance grants. These, however, are not policies which would get at the essential characteristics and underlying conditions of persistent unemployment outlined in the opening chapter. Much of frictional unemployment, especially in its more pathological forms, is an outgrowth of what are actually structural barriers to employment, and it is the elimination or reduction of these barriers to which public policy must be chiefly addressed.

Chapter 4
Reducing Structural Unemployment

Structural unemployment, the principal subject of this study, has been the source of much controversy partly because it defies clear-cut categorization. Indeed, some highly respected economists question the validity of the concept altogether, viewing all unemployment that is not the result of a deficiency in aggregate demand as falling in the frictional category.

Unemployment can be said to be structural in nature if aggregate demand is high enough to provide jobs at prevailing wages for everyone seeking work but job openings remain unfilled because of a persistent mismatching of skills or geographical locations. If the mismatching is resolved voluntarily through mutual search by workers and employers in a reasonably short period of time, say eight or ten weeks, the resulting unemployment falls in the frictional category. The unemployment becomes structural, however, if the mismatching cannot be resolved by such voluntary action and the job seekers are required to develop new skills or change their place of residence but are effectively precluded from doing so. In the former instance the workers choose to remain unemployed because of the likelihood, hopefully, of finding suitable work, while in the latter their unemployment is involuntary in the sense that they cannot overcome the barriers that bar them from such work.

The traditional view is that any unemployment resulting from mismatching *within* a given labor market, assuming an adequate level of aggregate demand, would be frictional in nature whereas it would be structural if the mismatching were *between* markets. While a useful distinction, it should be kept in mind that even within a given market, interferences and barriers having to do with lack of requisite skills, personal attributes, restrictive practices or even inadequate commuting facilities, may result in structural imbalances between buyers and sellers. The main point, however, is that even though job seekers may only be subject to frictional unemployment within a given market, they may be faced with structural unemployment between markets. While obviously not always precise, the distinction can be a crucially important one, particularly in the case of workers in the lowest skill, poorest paid occupations. Movement between jobs requiring little education, specialized training and prior work experience in a particular locality may only entail frictional unemployment in this sense, but if the workers are effectively confined to this relatively narrow, lowest skill type of work by reasons of barriers they have little or no hope of overcoming, structural unemployment, or more accurately, structural misallocation of employment, is present between markets. It is structural barriers resulting in misallocations of this sort which are of central importance to dealing with the problem of prosperity unemployment.

The unemployed inner city teenager who lacks basic educational skills and any meaningful work experience, or the one-time textile worker who has been left stranded in a New England town, are prototypes of this type of joblessness. But what of the Grade-A Machinist who cannot find work at his customary level but would do so if he were willing to accept a Grade-B classification or move to a distant city? Presumably the answer would turn on whether the barrier is surmountable by action of the individual involved, but this often involves a qualitative judgment. If opportunities are present to choose among a roughly homogeneous cluster of jobs, or to acquire the necessary qualifying skills and experience to do so within a feasible period of time, no structural component is involved; a structural component is only present when the means for making such choices, while perhaps available to some, are not available to others.

The clearest examples, of course, are those in which the two groups of job seekers are indistinguishable from one another except for some characteristic unrelated to actual job performance (color, sex, religion), but the exclusion can be basically structural even though performance-related differences are present if the means for overcoming or bypassing such differences are not available. Indeed, the principal feature of structural unemployment is not that certain workers are blocked from job opportunities within a specialized field of competence or limited geographical area but that they are effectively precluded from taking the necessary steps to gain access to a somewhat broader field or market area. While difficult to identify, this distinction is crucial to an understanding of structural unemployment.

A related source of ambiguity grows out of cost and productivity considerations. If particular workers are excluded from certain jobs even though cost and productivity comparisons are in their favor, a structural imbalance would seem evident. What if, however, the cost comparisons are unclear, or the excluded workers can be brought up to the productivity norm only after expensive training outlays are made, or the adverse cost comparisons are due to the attitudes of fellow workers, to considerations of plant morale, or other such semiobjective factors? In these circumstances, the important test is whether the excluded workers are given meaningful opportunities to prove their immediate and/or potential worth. If restrictive or screening procedures are adopted which, in effect, preclude certain workers from showing what they are capable of doing, a structural imbalance is involved since concrete evidence of their relatively poor performance or limited potential is lacking.

Even if there is such evidence, further questions need to be asked as to whether the resulting comparisons are themselves the product of basic structural barriers of one kind or another. From the viewpoint of the individual employer, the inferior-superior performance test may well be decisive unless offset by public subsidies, tax credits, and the like, but from the viewpoint of society, the issue of why this outcome occurred, and whether the personal or social benefits which would be derived from resolving the problem would outweigh the costs of doing so, still needs to be faced. Much would depend on the nature of the underlying imbalance—the deeper and more pervasive it is, the less likely corrective action would yield benefits in excess of costs. On the other hand, much would also depend on whether the society placed a high or low priority on the benefits sought (a problematic value judgment) and on whether the proposed corrective action would "work" (a problematic cost-benefit calculation). The difficulties posed by considerations of this sort need no underscoring.

Finally, while the unemployment resulting from structural imbalances is involuntary in nature, confusion often still arises as to where and how the line between voluntary and involuntary unemployment should be drawn. One variation of the traditional or classical view is that the major cause of a continuing imbalance in a given labor market is simply that the wage rate is being held above the equilibrium level and that if suppliers were willing to reduce their wage offers, or were forced by competition or other influences to do so, the imbalance would be removed. This variation marks an important departure from the more general traditional view, noted at the outset of this chapter, that all unemployment is the result either of inadequate aggregate demand or frictional influences, a view that rests on the assumption that labor markets, and indeed all markets, function under conditions of perfect competition; if it is assumed that noncompetitive conditions, whether imposed by workers, employers or government, are present, limiting unemployment to these two categories becomes quite unrealistic for no other reason than that the element of voluntary choice on the part of job seekers is not likely to be present.

Without attempting to settle this highly abstruse point here, it is clear that wage distortion can be a serious impediment to achieving a balanced condition in particular labor markets. In fact, from the viewpoint of those workers fortunate enough to keep their jobs, high, rigid wage rates can serve as an exclusionary device to prevent competitive bidding for any available openings by other workers, thereby perpetuating the favorable rates of pay. Whether this is a major source of structural unemployment is an issue taken up in the next chapter; the point emphasized here is that wage rates and related cost elements *can* be held at levels which, consciously or unconsciously, exclude certain workers from effectively bidding for jobs in just the same way as would outright bars to employment.

The other point deserving emphasis is that even though wage-distortion unemployment may in some sense be considered voluntarily induced, this is only likely to hold for very narrowly defined labor markets. Within such markets, as noted earlier, rapid turnover and frequent spells of unemployment can properly be viewed as voluntary, i.e., frictional, in nature. Between related markets or submarkets, however, the barriers to mobility are much less likely to be, in any meaningful sense, voluntarily maintained. If wage barriers are present, they are apt to be but external aspects of other types of market interferences, and it is only in this broader context that the relationships between wage costs and structural unemployment can be fully understood.

If effective steps are to be taken for dealing with this aspect of the prosperity unemployment problem, it is essential that the individuals involved be carefully identified so that their needs and abilities can be made clear. Given the complexities just described, however, it is hardly surprising that there is considerable confusion on this score. For one thing estimates of the extent of structural unemployment vary considerably depending on where the nonacceleration inflation level of unemployment is assumed to fall. According to Lloyd Reynolds, frictional unemployment at full employment can be assumed to be about 4 percent, and structural unemployment about 1 percent, of the nation's civilian labor force, with unfilled vacancies also amounting to about 1 percent of the labor force and the rate of price increase holding steady at roughly 5 percent per annum.[1] In terms of 1980 labor force projections, this would yield an estimate of only a little over 1 million structurally unemployed.

Efforts to build up an estimate from major categories of structural unemployment are more firmly based but are still open to question. The first category consists of the long term unemployed; if this category is defined to include workers unemployed 27 weeks or more, there were only about 300,000 structurally unemployed workers (roughly three-tenths of 1 percent of the civilian labor force) in the high employment year of 1973, but if the definition is limited to workers unemployed only 15 weeks or more, the total comes to about 800,000, roughly 1 percent of that year's civilian labor force. In the somewhat less prosperous year of 1978,

1. Reynolds, *Labor Economics and Labor Relations,* p. 132.

the group unemployed 27 weeks or more came to a little over 1 percent, and the group unemployed 15 weeks or more to nearly 2.5 percent, of the 1978 civilian labor force.[2]

The second category consists of discouraged workers, those who have dropped out of the labor force because they have lost all hope of finding any suitable work. This type of unmeasured (as opposed to measured) unemployment, however, is associated almost wholly with periods of cyclical downswing and persistent business slack, not with periods of rising business and general prosperity. Indeed, in the latter periods the overall supply of labor increases rapidly as many persons who had previously not been working, chiefly women and teenagers, enter the labor force in search of employment. In the Vietnam War years between 1963 and 1967, for example, it has been estimated that the additional workers drawn into the labor force totaled 1.9 million, of whom more than a million were women. Similarly, in the relatively prosperous years 1967-1971, the proportion of total unemployment accounted for by discouraged workers has been put at substantially less than 1 percent of the civilian labor force.[3] At a 5-6 percent level of unemployment it seems unlikely that, out of a total labor force of 100 million, more than 700,000 would fall in the discouraged category.

Still a third category consists of part time workers who want full time work but cannot find it because of economic conditions. Since these workers do have jobs but are involuntarily limited to less than full time work, the generally accepted procedure is to consider such workers as only half

---

2. *Employment and Training Report of the President, 1979* (Washington: Government Printing Office, 1980), Appendix Tables A-1 and A-26.

3. William G. Bowen and T. Aldrich Finegan, *The Economics of Labor Force Participation* (Princeton, NJ: Princeton University Press, 1969); Jacob Mincer, "Determining Who Are the Hidden Unemployed," *Monthly Labor Review,* 96 (1973), pp. 27-30.

unemployed.[4] Again, as in the case of the discouraged category, this type of unemployment becomes relatively unimportant in periods of general prosperity; in 1978, for example, it amounted to less than a fifth of a percentage point of the civilian labor force (see table 4-1).[5]

The fourth and last category consists of workers who are involuntarily confined to low-level, unstable jobs and as a consequence have only intermittent work even in periods of high employment. Unfortunately, there are no published statistics on the extent of this type of work since the problem of measurement is virtually insurmountable. Many of the workers having these highly unstable jobs, especially white women over 20 years of age and white teenagers, hold intermittent jobs of this sort voluntarily in the sense they face other virtually equivalent options and remain outside the unemployed category in the official figures. On the other hand, many others, especially nonwhites, have intermittent work and still fall within the official definition of measured unemployment in a given year. While adequate data are lacking, there is little doubt that the uncounted portion of the "virtually unemployed" is of significant size even in periods of general prosperity.

Summarizing the available evidence, estimates of the total number of the structurally unemployed at the general jobless level of 5 percent fall between 2.5 and 3.5 million depending in large part on whether long term unemployment is defined as 15 weeks or more as against 27 weeks or more. However the outlook is viewed, it is evident that the problem of structural unemployment will continue to be a formidable one even in periods of high employment. It is no less clear that any attack on the problem, to be effective, calls for breaking

---

4. Julius Shiskin, "Employment and Unemployment: The Doughnut or the Hole?" *Monthly Labor Review* (February 1976), pp. 3-10.

5. *Employment and Training Report of the President, 1979,* Table A-33.

Table 4-1
Categories of Unemployment, Selected Years 1973-78

	Thousands			Percent of Civilian Labor Force		
	1973	1975	1978	1973	1975	1978
Civilian Labor Force	88.7	92.6	100.0			
Total unemployed	4.3	7.8	6.0	4.9	8.5	6.0
Unemployed 15 weeks and over	.8	2.5	1.4	.9	2.6	1.4
Unemployed 27 weeks and over	.3	1.2	.6	.3	1.3	.6
1/2 of unemployed part-time for economic reasons	1.3	1.9	1.7	1.5	2.0	1.7
Discouraged workers at 5 percent unemployment	--	--	.7	--	--	.7

Source: Employment and Training Report of the President, 1979, Tables A-1, A-26 and A-33.

down this large demographic group into smaller, more homogeneous categories. While the preceding discussion has gone some distance in identifying the structurally unemployed and the severely disadvantaged employed, the workers involved form too large and ill-defined a group for policymaking purposes; further decomposition is therefore necessary even though quantitative estimates of their relative size are not possible.

The three groups who chiefly make up the structurally unemployed—teenagers, women and adult males with serious background deficiencies, particularly the nonwhite and other minority members of these three groups—possess a wide diversity of characteristics and capacities. The same holds true of other workers who confront special job finding difficulties and who form a fringe around these main groups: those 20-24 years old, those over 55 years old, the physically handicapped, and workers in isolated, depressed areas. For policy to be effective, attention needs to be given to the ways in which each of these groups is affected by the various barriers limiting employment opportunities of the hard-to-employ. This study is largely confined to the first three of the groups just mentioned.

Four Barriers Confronting the Structurally Unemployed

The structurally unemployed are subject to a number of different barriers, some serious and at least in the short run quite irremovable, others much less difficult to surmount. The most important of these barriers are four in number: impediments to competitive wage determination and disincentives to work associated with nonwork sources of income; discrimination in hiring and promotion procedures; deficiencies in general education and in job or career training; and finally, lack of work experience. For policymaking purposes the most pressing need is to consider these four barriers both individually and as a group with a view to determining as clearly and as objectively as possible what is the relative importance of each and how each can be most effectively approached.

The first barrier, distortions in wage rates and impediments to effective job search, is easily explained, more difficult to identify and extremely hard to remedy. The assumption underlying this view of structural unemployment is that many of the hard-to-employ are quite ready and prepared to take on the responsibilities of a job but are discouraged or blocked from doing so by a variety of noncompetitive, or explicitly anticompetitive, impediments: inflexibly high wage rates, restrictive hiring and promotion standards, overly generous inducements not to work and the like. It follows from this view that structural unemployment would be substantially lessened if these limitations on competitive labor market behavior could be removed.

The second barrier, discriminatory labor market behavior, is far more complex and intractable than the first but at the same time much closer to underlying factors that give rise to structural unemployment. Sometimes it takes a clear, unmistakable form but more frequently it is intermixed with quite defensible purposes or needs; sometimes it is closely correlated with differences in worker efficiency, but more often the relationship to efficiency differences is extremely loose; even where efficiency differs, the effects of such prior "institutional" forms of discrimination as inadequate schooling or particular family backgrounds are clearly evident but extremely difficult to pin down. Since labor market discrimination has so many facets and is so deeply imbedded in historical developments and social attitudes, quick results from any effort to attack structural unemployment by this route can hardly be expected.

The third barrier, deficiencies in general education and in training in specific skill of job requirements, poses less difficulties than discriminatory labor market behavior, but far more difficulties than restrictive wage practices and job search disincentives. If structural unemployment were largely limited to experienced workers who have been displaced by technological or other market developments, the assumption which largely underlay the government's manpower programs of the late 1950s and early 1960s, the difficulties besetting the general education-specific training route would have been far less. Since it is now clear that this type of unemployment centers on persons who lack fundamental educational and work skills, the hurdles are seen to be far more formidable. Recent experience, as the subsequent discussion shows, points to certain promising lines of action, but the overall prospect is hardly reassuring.

The fourth and final barrier, closely related to the one just noted, is lack of prior work experience. This is the most important immediate hurdle which new entrants to the labor market, notably teenagers just out of school, confront, but it also poses serious difficulties for adult women and older men who are seeking reentry to the labor market after long absences. It is sometimes argued that almost any kind of job, whatever its content, duration or source, can provide an essential first step in dealing with this barrier, but if the work is for only brief periods and makes little or no substantive demands, it is unlikely to provide any meaningful entry or reentry preparation. At least it is clear that for persons from severely disadvantaged backgrounds, work at this lowest level often proves to be dead-end in terms of any career potential. Thus for such persons it is now recognized that job experience alone, even if it entails some substantive elements, rarely provides entry to any longer term career opportunities.

A Possible Overall Strategy

All of the structurally unemployed face at least one of these four barriers and some, notably nonwhite teenagers, face all four. The critical issue confronting policymakers is how to devise an effective set of programs which can be adapted to the different and changing needs of these various groups. The closer the individual is to being fully job-ready, the more straightforward and immediate the policy approach can be; the further removed the individual is, the more complex and long term the policy has to be.

Before turning to an analysis of specific policy issues, the question of how an approach along these lines can best be adapted to an environment of business expansion and high employment needs to be faced. As a starting point it is worth emphasizing that in any broad and sustained business expansion, increasing numbers of job opportunities at entry level and above are opening up for a widening spectrum of job seekers. Special measures are still required to bring the different structurally employed groups into the mainstream of employment opportunities, but the policies can be more limited and more closely linked to usual market requirements than in recessionary or even sluggish expansionist periods.

This not only means that such policies will be likelier to succeed in these circumstances but also as a practical matter that the test of meeting competitive, regular work requirements in the private and public sector will become applicable to increasing numbers of the structurally unemployed. Likewise, as business conditions improve, the role of the private as opposed to the public sector can be expected to become increasingly important. This is not, however, a policy emphasis that can be adopted abruptly. Even in relatively strong expansions, special demand supports will be needed to meet the job needs of these different unemployment-prone groups.

Adapting such a strategy to structurally unemployed workers would entail difficult and controversial borderline decisions, but on both macro-stability and micro-efficiency grounds, the shift in policy emphasis indicated by an expansionist environment seems clear and compelling. Under conditions of general prosperity those workers who by reason of skill and experience are most job ready would increasingly be able to find openings with a minimum of assistance. In such cases, specialized training in a new skill, for example, or removal of an entry barrier to a particular line of work, would be all that would be necessary.

For those further removed from entry into regular work, considerably more effort would need to be expended in determining what barriers are involved and in carrying through effective support actions. Thus, for some, the difficulty may have to do with a basic educational deficiency, for others with personal family problems, for still others with lack of physical proximity to any job opportunities. Once carefully examined and assessed, the difficulties besetting job seekers in this intermediate group are apt to be relatively clear-cut since persons in this category possess the basic motivations and innate capacities to handle regular jobs. The benefits deriving from any supportive action, however, will probably take considerably longer to realize than in the case of the first group of job seekers because of the differing nature and scope of their difficulties.

Those in the third category, the still less job-ready group, are not only likely to confront at least some of the barriers facing the first two groups but also to lack essential psychological or intellectual attributes needed for regular employment. In their case, any effective remedial action will doubtless entail more long term, individualized treatment. Unless society were to decide to accept the risks and costs of disregarding the special needs of job seekers in this group, much preparatory effort would be required before they could move into regular work situations, and each of the preparatory steps would need to be closely monitored. The uncertainties and difficulties besetting any serious effort along these lines need no underscoring.

The final category are those workers who are subject to various types of discriminatory labor market practices. Since these practices are generally interwoven with such other factors as hiring test procedures, wage progression structures, and educational requirements, most of the workers subject to labor market discrimination are also in one or more of the other groups that are vulnerable to structural unemployment. Nonetheless, this aspect of their disadvantaged status warrants separate attention in any canvas of possible policy approaches.

Under conditions of high employment, then, the case for greatly narrowing the focus of government efforts to deal with structural unemployment becomes very strong. These efforts could proceed along the following lines: first, identify those workers who are most in need, presumably chiefly on income-level grounds; second, group these workers by their degree of readiness to enter a career or to do regular work; and third, tailor the various subsidized training jobs and related approaches that now exist to the special needs and circumstances of each group. The important distinction to keep in mind is that in a high employment environment, a massive governmental attack on structural unemployment would be inappropriate; rather it would be more realistic to limit public effort to those workers in this category who can benefit from training and special work programs, relying on welfare or other forms of assistance to meet the needs of those who cannot meet this standard. Added perspective is given to these recommendations when viewed against the experience of other industrialized countries.

The West European Experience

In most respects, a public policy approach to structural unemployment along these lines would differ quite sharply from the pattern followed by most West European governments. Outwardly, the differences are not striking; as in this country, their programs are built around labor market information systems, job placement and counseling, career training and development, subsidies to induce private employers to hire the hard-to-employ, and job creation aids largely oriented towards depressed areas and economically disadvantaged groups. The underlying thrust of the West European programs, however, has been quite different. Until recently, government efforts to deal with unemployment in this country have centered almost entirely on aggregative demand policies, with scant attention to removing structural barriers to employment. In the case of most West European countries, the overall unemployment rate has until recent years held well below the American rate, even to the point where large numbers of foreign workers have been brought in to meet unfilled demands. In those countries, such non-frictional unemployment as existed was clearly structural in nature, calling for intensive, highly individualized support measures in the case of very severely disadvantaged workers, and broad training or human development measures in the case of less disadvantaged groups. As a result, the overall coverage of their structural policies is considerably broader than in this country, eligibility requirements for participation are less stringent, and the content of their programs is more diverse and far-reaching.

The other striking difference grows out of the greater centralization of authority that has developed in West European countries both within major industries and with respect to the powers exercised by their central governments. Historically, there has emerged a much higher degree of coordination between employer and union policies than in this country, as well as a greater acceptance of government participation and leadership in the formulation of such policies. This has meant that the hard-to-employ are not treated as a group apart from the working population as a whole, the pattern prevailing in the United States, but rather as one of many groups needing special aids and general development measures. It is too early to judge whether the West European countries will meet the recent increase in their unemployment rolls by expanding these same human resource programs or by resorting to more sweeping aggregate demand measures, but the evidence to date suggests that they will hold to the former course.[6]

---

6. *Recent European Manpower Initiatives, Special Report No. 3* (Washington: National Commission for Manpower Policy, 1975).

Should this country adopt essentially the same approach as West Europe to structural unemployment? Clearly, the differences in the two environments, both economic and social, are too great to make any such outcome possible. If the major recommendations developed in this study were adopted, however, American policy would move a considerable distance towards the West European pattern, the focus as at present remaining on the needs of the hard-to-employ but only as part of a more comprehensive and long range program of human resources development.

Five Policy Approaches

Public policy approaches to these four barriers are proceeding along five main lines, with some approaches overlapping others in relation to a particular barrier. Even where a given approach is limited to a single barrier, it is now generally agreed, the results to date have at best been mixed. In at least a few instances, however, the criticisms appear to be too extreme.

Policy efforts addressed to the first barrier, formal and informal noncompetitive impediments to job entry and work disincentives resulting from unemployment insurance and other income support programs, are beset with innumerable uncertainties and controversies in determining when such restrictions and practices are and are not justified. The second policy approach, an outgrowth of the national effort to protect the civil rights of all the nation's citizens, is aimed at reducing and eliminating discriminatory barriers to employment, especially as they relate to women and minority groups. Recent experience indicates that the antidiscriminatory approach to the structural unemployment issue is beset with serious difficulties, raising the question of whether efforts in this direction, whatever their merits on other grounds, can ever provide a successful focus for effective action against structural unemployment.

There remain three other major approaches: efforts to strengthen educational-vocational preparation for work careers, direct job creation efforts in the public and private sector, and finally, public and private training programs in specific skills and related job requirements. Each of these last three approaches typically contains elements of basic employment preparation, direct job training and work experience in various combinations and, taken together, have a direct or indirect bearing on all four of the barriers noted earlier. While each warrants separate discussion, in policy terms they have become so closely interrelated they form a single group; as such, they constitute the country's major thrust in dealing with structural unemployment among the seriously disadvantaged. The remainder of this study is addressed to an assessment of these five approaches to the problem.

Chapter 5
Noncompetitive and Work Disincentive Barriers

The simplest and in many ways most intellectually appealing explanation of unemployment in periods of general prosperity can be traced to traditional competitive market analysis. According to this view, if labor in a given market remains unemployed at existing wage rates, adjustments in those rates will insure that everyone looking for work will eventually find it, assuming incomes are determined by competitive conditions alone. If such conditions do not obtain, either noncompetitive restrictions or nonmarket determinants of income are presumably involved and may well call for corrective action.

Noncompetitive barriers in labor markets, the first of these two influences, take many forms. Union restrictions in the hiring and placement of workers may impede freedom of entry. Requirements in the way of prior experience and training may be set so high that many qualified job applicants are effectively excluded. Costs associated with private pension programs, health plans and other fringe protections, quite aside from similar benefits required by law, may also discourage new hires. High, rigid wage rates, whether posted by public or private action, can have a similar effect on job entry.

Behind these direct impediments lie many more indirect and roundabout forms of interferences with competitive access to job opportunities, including collusive price and market strategies of employers and government regulations which restrict competitive adjustments in rates and costs. Merely to enumerate some of the more important barriers that may develop in labor and related markets is enough to show how difficult any action along these lines, to be at all effective, must be. In good part, this follows from the fact that the results of such action, especially as they relate to structural unemployment, would probably not be evident for long periods of time. Indeed, other developments might well occur that would obscure their impact altogether.

Moreover, what may seem to be an arbitrary and unwarranted restriction to a job applicant may appear to an employer or union as essential to maintaining minimum standards of performance or to meeting widely accepted criteria of equity. A limitation that was once needed, as in the 1930s, to prevent the complete demoralization of an industry's system of wage rates and working conditions may be rendered economically indefensible by subsequent shifts in production methods or consumer preferences. More important, restrictions on job entry are apt to be the product of powerful but narrow group interests whose first obligations are to their own members. Exclusion of newcomers, if needed to preserve hard-won gains, would therefore appear to these groups to be quite appropriate if not absolutely necessary.

In the face of these difficulties and uncertainties it is hard to see how this approach could be used as the center piece of any successful program for dealing with structural unemployment. Even if, for example, wage rate distortions could be shown to be a major cause of this type of unemployment, what criteria would be used to determine where and how such distortions should be rectified? If wage rigidities in certain industries, such as basic steel or chemicals, are part and parcel of an industry's system of pricing and marketing practices, would it be either sensible or feasible to limit remedial action to the wage element alone? If a broader strategy were pursued, would the effects filter through to affect job opportunity levels in any significant way? Concerted attacks on even relatively clear-cut barriers to job entry such as high fringe benefit levels, excessive hiring or performance standards, and direct labor supply restrictions would pose hardly less serious difficulties.

In deciding on any course of action along these lines, attention needs to focus on those impediments to job entry which bear most heavily on the hardest-to-employ groups but which at the same time are most likely to yield to policy intervention in periods of general prosperity. Much attention of late has been given to possible adverse effects on employment of increases under the federal minimum wage law. Since this impediment bears directly on the job prospects of major groups of the structurally unemployed, it warrants attention here.

Federal Minimum Wage Legislation

Ever since passage of the Fair Labor Standards Act of 1938, controversy has continued about the possible dislocating effects of setting a national minimum wage. Initially the law set the basic rate at 25 cents per hour with time and a half for any work over 40 hours per week. The latter provision still obtains but the basic minimum has been periodically raised and in 1980 stood at $3.10 an hour. Under recent legislative action, the rate is scheduled to rise to $3.31 an hour by 1981.

Equally important, coverage since the 1930s has been greatly expanded to include large numbers of workers in retail trade, services, agriculture and domestic work as well as all nonsupervisory employees of federal, state and local governments. The potential employment effects of raising the national wage minimum has obviously become more serious as the coverage of the law has been widened to include more low-wage workers. The 1966 amendment, for example, extended coverage to an additional 8 million retail, hospital, hotel, restaurant, laundry and construction employees, while the 1974 amendment brought 1.5 million domestic workers and half a million additional retail and service workers under the protection of the law. These fields include many traditionally low-paying firms that hire low-skilled workers, many of them teenagers and nonwhites who have little work experience and who suffer relatively high rates of unemployment. In total numbers, the 1974 amendment extended the Act's coverage to some 56 million workers.

Two major criticisms are leveled against this legislation: first, it heightens inflationary pressures and second, it results in increased unemployment. The former issue, which can be touched on only briefly in this study, has received much attention in recent years but little in the way of systematic analysis.[1] Such work as has been done indicates that the effects of increases in the federal minimum wage on the general price level have until recently been practically indiscernible but that in the economic environment of the 1970s this has become less true. As noted in chapter 2, the spread of government regulations, including those which induce wage increases, has tended to make any inflation, once underway, more persistent. In early 1978, for example, wage increases accelerated markedly, though briefly, at a time when unemployment was still somewhat above 6 percent. In

---

1. Two long term projects sponsored by the American Enterprise Institute for Public Policy Research and the U.S. Department of Labor should help meet the latter need.

its analysis of this development, the Council of Economic Advisers concluded that the 15 percent rise in the minimum wage which occurred in January 1978 raised the rate of increase of the adjusted hourly earnings index from 7.9 percent to 9.2 percent on an annual basis; the other main factor to which it attributed most of the upswing in the pace of wage increases in early 1978 was the *speed* in the increase in total employment along with the equally rapid drop in unemployment. For 1978 as a whole, compensation per hour went up from a 7.6 percent increase in 1977 to a 9.8 percent rate in 1978. This step-up in the pace of wage increases, combined with a continued slowdown in the rate of increase in productivity, resulted in a substantial rise in unit labor costs, with the rate of increase of such costs in the private nonfarm sector rising from 6.3 percent in 1977 to 8.9 percent in 1978.[2] These factors, among which the higher minimum was clearly visible if not central for the year as a whole, served to push up prices still higher and helped imbed the inflationary process more deeply into the economy.

The conclusion seems inescapable that any serious effort to lessen inflationary pressures will require a significantly lower rate of increase in minimum wages than is provided under existing legislation. It also is evident that, to be effective, any such move would need to be coupled with similar cutbacks in a wide variety of other government regulations including: reductions in protective tariffs in steel, textiles and the like; elimination of regulations in trucking, shipping and communications; relaxation of price supports in agriculture and in subsidies for the maritime industry; and the dismantling of many other cost-raising types of government interventions. Similar questions have been raised about government controls aimed at protecting not particular pro-

---

2. *Economic Report of the President, 1979* (Washington: Government Printing Office, 1980), pp. 52 and 66.

ducer groups but the more general public such as those dealing with environmental pollution, dangerous food additives and occupational hazards. In their case, the issues become far more complex, however, because of the important social benefits which these public-oriented types of regulations are felt to entail. The fact remains that if a broad scale attack on inflation is mounted, the rapid pace of increase in the minimum wage rate of the past few years would have to be reduced.

The second line of criticism, that this legislation has barred hard-to-employ groups from jobs, bears directly on the problem of structural unemployment. In this regard, there is now virtual unanimity among investigators on two somewhat conflicting points: first, whatever other benefits may derive from this legislation, any substantial *increase* in the minimum wage relative to the general wage level tends to reduce employment opportunities for the least skilled and the least experienced; second, however, any decrease in the minimum wage relative to the general wage level, unless it were quite substantial, would have little effect on job opportunities for the hard-to-employ. The first point is especially applicable to periods of business contraction when demand for labor is generally shifting downward relative to supply while the second is most clearly evident in periods of business expansion. Both points, however, are by-products of the same underlying principle: the level of job openings for the least skilled, least experienced workers are far more dependent on overall demand-supply conditions than on changes in the relative wage rate for this type of work. In expansions, the job finding prospects of such workers will largely turn on whether the rise in aggregate demand reaches a level at which employers are induced to take them on in substantial numbers. Contrariwise, their job finding difficulties in periods of general decline will largely turn on how far aggregate demand falls below aggregate supply. In neither instance, barring the most extreme hypothetical assumptions, will a change in relative wages significantly alter the outcome.

This leaves one general circumstance when the wage for this type of labor relative to other types has major employment effects, i.e., when longer term supply-demand conditions for the least skilled, least experienced workers become markedly adverse. In this kind of a setting, employers face a more or less permanent rise in the relative cost of hiring such workers if their wage is forced upward through legislative action. This is what has been happening for much of the past 25 years. As often pointed out, this has been especially true of the 1970s when a sharp rise in the number of women and young people seeking jobs coincided with a marked slowdown in the longer term growth rate of the economy. The subsequent rise in unemployment among these hard-to-employ groups was largely the result of these two developments. The increases in the federal minimum wage which occurred during this period, while apparently not a major causal influence, aggravated an already difficult condition.

Empirical Findings

Of the many statistical studies that have been made of the employment effects of increases in the minimum wage, almost all conclude that this legislation has made it more difficult for teenagers, nonwhites generally, and perhaps women to find work opportunities. At the same time, the majority of these studies conclude that other factors are considerably more important in explaining the relatively high unemployment level among these groups.

One of the earliest studies to emphasize the adverse employment effects of minimum wage legislation was conducted by Arthur F. Burns; he found that an increase of 25 cents in the statutory legal minima is associated with a rise of 8 percentage points in nonwhite unemployment.[3] In a later study, Jacob Mincer concluded, "No more than a third of the employment loss in the covered sector appears as unemployment, while the bulk withdraws from the labor force."[4] He found that the largest disemployment effects are observed for nonwhite teenagers, followed by nonwhite males (20-24), white teenagers, and white males (20-24).

In a careful review of a variety of statistical studies of this problem and his own analysis of the data, Edward Gramlich concluded that a 25 percent increase in the minimum wage would lower employment of low-wage teenagers (those receiving less than the minimum before the increase in question) by 10-15 percent. Comparable effects would presumably be felt by other workers who had previously been receiving wages below the minimum. The impact would be substantially less on teenager employment as a whole or on other groups that are particularly prone to unemployment.[5]

Except in the case of very marked increases, changes in the minimum wage have apparently had only minimal disemployment effects. This is due in good part to the fact that, while a higher minimum has had adverse effects on teenager employment, it has been followed by a *rise* in the number of full time jobs for women, suggesting that in these circumstances employers substitute unskilled women for teenagers. This is worth noting since women represent

---

3. Arthur F. Burns, *The Management of Prosperity* (New York: Columbia University Press, 1966), p. 48.

4. Jacob Mincer, "Unemployment Effects of Minimum Wages," *Journal of Political Economy* (August 1976), pp. 87-106.

5. Edward M. Gramlich, *Impact of Minimum Wages on Other Wages, Employment, and Family Incomes,* Brookings Papers on Economic Activity, 2 (1976), pp. 409-451. For a convenient summary of recent studies, see American Enterprise Institute for Public Policy Research, *Minimum Wage Legislation* (Washington 1977).

roughly half of all low-wage workers, outnumbering teenagers in that category by a ratio of about 5 to 3.[6]

In terms of policy choices, the critical relationship involved is the national minimum as a ratio to the average wage level or, what is often used in its place, to the average wage in manufacturing. This ratio, as indicated in Figure 5-1, has usually varied between 40 and 50 percent. As long as the national minimum is held towards the lower end of this range, few serious employment effects seem likely, but as it approaches the upper end, employment opportunities for low-paid workers, especially teenagers, would become fewer. While far short of a cure-all, there is little question but what the employment situation of teenagers and perhaps other low-wage workers would have been at least somewhat better if the increases in the minimum wage had been kept lower than those recently enacted. The case for these increases must therefore be made on other than employment-expansion grounds for the structurally unemployed.

These empirical findings, while generally supportive of the position that minimum wage legislation has been a relatively unimportant factor in explaining structural unemployment in this country, do not of themselves settle the issue one way or the other. There are further considerations, however, which go a long way towards doing so.

First, prospective population trends over the next 10-15 years should gradually alter the unemployment problem among the hard-to-employ, especially young persons. The last of the postwar baby boom will pass through their teenage years by 1981 and the youth population will decline thereafter in relative and absolute terms through the 1980s.

---

6. Gramlich, *Impact of Minimum Wages,* p. 443.

Figure 5-1
Level of Minimum Wage

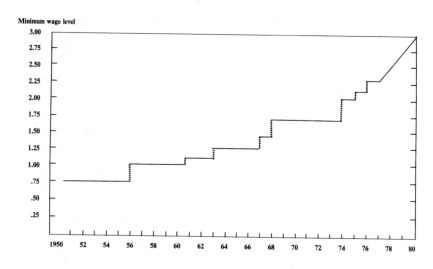

Minimum wage level

Minimum as Percentage of Average Wage in Manufacturing

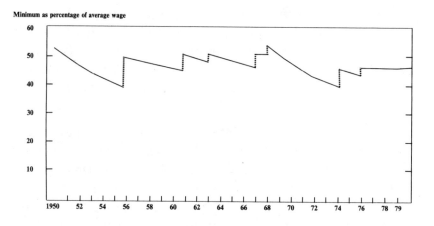

Minimum as percentage of average wage

Source: Adapted from American Enterprise Institute for Public Policy Research, Minimum Wage Legislation, p. 2; and Peyton K. Elder and Heide D. Miller, "The Fair Labor Standards Act: Changes of Four Decades," *Monthly Labor Review* (July 1979), p.11.

In summarizing the projected trends, Adams and Mangum concluded:

The effect of this influx of young people, however, has already begun to dissipate and will largely disappear in the 1980s. The teenage labor force, in turn, is expected to decline from its level of 8.8 million to 7.9 million in 1985.[7]

This puts the issue of the employment effect of the minimum wage in a quite different light. During the 1960s and 1970s the ratio of youth to adult unemployment nearly doubled from its base of three to one which obtained during the 1950s. By 1975, the ratio of youth to adult unemployment already appeared to have returned to its historical base. The structural element in youth unemployment of course still remains, but any adverse effects attributable to minimum wage legislation have now been substantially removed and may soon disappear altogether.

Second, it can still be argued that the minimum wage has adverse employment effects with respect to particular low-wage groups such as young nonwhites, women or indeed any group whose wage is below the statutory minimum. This argument applies especially to young nonwhites since their numbers will decline only slightly during the 1980s and there is every indication their unemployment rate will remain inordinately high.

A closer look at the labor force status of these different groups, however, raises serious questions about this line of analysis. With respect to women, for example, there is no evidence that their employment status has worsened as a result of the minimum wage; in fact, as already noted, it appears that the number of full time jobs for women has been

---

7. Arvil V. Adams and Garth L. Mangum, *The Lingering Crisis of Youth Unemployment* (Kalamazoo, MI: W.E. Upjohn Institute for Employment Research, 1978), p. 127.

increased rather than decreased by this legislation as employers have substituted unskilled women for teenagers.[8]

As to young people generally, it is important to remember that, while over 40 percent are employed in any given year, the great majority are enrolled in school and any work they do consists of temporary jobs during the summer combined with part time work during the school year. The adverse effects of the minimum wage on such persons, if in fact they occur, constitute a far less serious cost than if they were full time workers. Unemployment among the latter group, especially among nonwhites in inner-city areas, poses extremely serious problems, but that the minimum wage is a major impediment even in their case seems unlikely. Lowering the minimum wage would cut across the entire range of low-wage labor, not just young, out-of-school job seekers, so the latter would still be at the end of the labor queue in competing for available openings. Proposals to establish a special lower minimum rate for this particularly hard-to-employ group deserve consideration but, administrative difficulties aside, there is little evidence to indicate that merely reducing the applicable rate would alter their employment status to any significant degree. For young school dropouts, especially nonwhites in inner-city areas, the barriers to employment are the product of a complex of factors including deficiencies in skill training, basic educational preparation and inadequate work experience, to say nothing of employer flight from particular localities and the general deterioration of whole inner-city areas. At the very least, even if a lower special group rate were established, emphasis would still need to be placed on dealing with these more fundamental factors.

Third, as suggested above, an effective attack on the problems of hard-core unemployment has to be carefully

---

8. Gramlich, *Impact of Minimum Wages,* p. 443.

tailored to the needs of the particular groups involved with sufficiently concentrated, sustained efforts regarding the most hard-to-employ to make meaningful outcomes possible. What the specific ingredients of such an approach would be is impossible to say if for no other reason than because of the varying characteristics of the different groups involved. The element common to the members of all these groups, however, is an inability to meet and maintain minimum performance standards of employers, whether in the private or public sector. In a very short-run sense, the wage is of course one determinant involved, but the principal barrier in a more basic sense is a lack of essential employable qualities. Indeed, this is precisely the factor that distinguishes the hard-to-employ from other unemployed groups. It follows that any program that does not make this factor its primary focus cannot hope to succeed.

The foregoing considerations apply with special force in periods of business expansion and rising employment. The main hope for the hard-to-employ acquiring stable jobs is in such periods which in turn makes it doubly important they can qualify for such openings as they develop. Seen in this light, emphasis on the applicable wage, whether determined by legislative action or other means, has little relevance to the central issues involved.

Work Disincentive Barriers

Increasing attention has been given in recent years to the charge that an important part of structural unemployment is attributable to government policies, particularly with respect to unemployment insurance and various assistance programs. This is said to follow from the fact that these programs make it possible for workers to "go on the dole" instead of taking whatever jobs are available. As recent investigations make clear, this turns out to be a most complicated issue, making any sweeping conclusion impossible. Only a few of the most important findings can be noted here.

There is no question but what government income support programs tend to discourage job seeking and job holding among groups that are particularly subject to structural unemployment. Common sense leads to no other conclusion. If someone can receive a monthly check without working that is larger or even merely somewhat smaller than what could be gotten from working, why bother to look for a job? The issue, then, is how much of the country's unemployment can be attributed to this feature of the government's income support system.

A full answer to this question would require a detailed review of the present system of income supports in relation to incomes received from working and an analysis of how workers respond to this relationship under different circumstances. Before considering the unemployment insurance and public assistance programs in these terms, some general observations are worth noting.

As in most other aspects of the structural unemployment problem, the nature of this issue is greatly altered when the economy moves from low to high unemployment. When jobs become scarce and those that exist are not likely to last long, nonwork sources of income become the principal means of livelihood for increasing numbers of people. Inducements to seek out job openings decline while incentives to "stretch the rules" and qualify for some type of income support program become greater. The opposite tends to occur when job openings multiply and the unemployment rate falls. This is not to say that such programs do not aggravate the jobless problem in periods of low unemployment; in fact, their *relative* importance increases at such times because most of the unemployment that remains in prosperities is of a frictional and structural nature, the types of unemployment most directly affected by income support programs. Nonetheless, it becomes far easier to prevent abuses of these programs when jobs are plentiful than when they are scarce.

Much controversy, however, exists over what constitutes abuses of the present system of supports and how far society should go in preventing them. Is a mother who is the sole support of a couple of children under the age of six, or even ten or twelve, "abusing" the public assistance program by choosing to stay home rather than take a job? Is a person on unemployment insurance who holds out for a job offer at a wage rate comparable to what was received on the last job guilty of malingering? How detailed and intensive should government investigative efforts be in tracking down those who no longer qualify for benefits? The answers to these and similar questions turn largely on personal values and social outlooks, making clear that the country's income support programs will remain controversial simply because they reflect such a variety of personal views.

Any assessment of the effects on unemployment of these programs will largely depend on whether the issue is approached from the viewpoint of achieving more competitive labor market conditions or, alternatively, from the viewpoint of achieving a higher minimum level of income for everyone, another instance of the perennial conflict between efficiency and equity. If efficient allocation of labor is the goal, the case for severely limiting the coverage of income support programs as well as the level and duration of benefits becomes very strong. If a "decent" minimum living standard for all is the goal, the associated costs of inefficient labor markets may well seem acceptable.

In recent years, however, a rather different approach to income support programs has emerged which should go some way at least towards reconciling these two objectives. According to this view, such programs need not necessarily discourage job seeking or work effort as long as care is taken to insure that incomes are significantly increased from working, even if some part of a person's income still comes from nonwork sources. Controversy continues over how high the income support minimum should be, how much net gain from working should be allowed, where the cutoff in support payments should come as incomes rise, and how much pressure or coercion should be brought to bear on "able-bodied" relief recipients to take jobs, but the basic idea of combining income supports and work incentives is now widely accepted. These considerations apply particularly to the country's welfare programs, which are taken up in the concluding section of this chapter, but they also have an important bearing on the possible work disincentive effects of the nation's unemployment insurance system.

Unemployment Compensation System

The country's first line of defense against the hardships associated with unemployment is the federal-state unemployment compensation system established under the Social Security Act of 1935. Historically, coverage was limited primarily to industrial and commercial workers, but protection has since been extended to include agricultural workers, domestics, and other groups as well. At the same time, as wages generally have increased, benefit levels have been raised through cooperative federal-state action. Even excluding the extra unemployment compensation attributable to the 1973-1975 recession, unemployment benefits rose from $3 billion in 1965 to $9 billion in 1977.

The major purpose and effect of the law is to lessen the impact of unemployment on those who involuntarily lose their jobs by providing them with cash benefits (usually about 50 percent of prior earnings) for relatively brief periods (usually about 25 weeks, though Congress has been quick to extend benefits during periods of rising unemployment).[9] One of the principal advantages of the system is that it is automatically countercyclical to the extent that benefits paid out increase in recessions and decline in expansions. Thus between 1973 and 1975 the number of first benefit recipients rose from about 5 to 11 million and total benefits from about $4 to $12 billion.[10] It has been estimated that unemployment insurance has cushioned about 10 percent of the declines in GNP that have occurred since 1948 and that the unemployment rate would have risen 3.63 percentage points, as against the actual rise of about 3.3 points that occurred on average during these periods.[11] This estimate assumes that even though the taxes on employer payrolls that finance unemployment benefits tend to move *procyclically,* since in most states they are tied to individual company performance by the so-called merit rating mechanism, the tax rate adjustments involved occur too slowly to have much of a destabilizing effect. While the main countercyclical effect of unemployment benefits was felt in recessions, especially steep recessions, this meant that the unemployment rate in the subsequent expansion periods was also probably somewhat less.

In recent years, a number of economists, notably Arthur Burns and Martin Feldstein, have argued that certain features of the unemployment insurance system have an adverse effect on the unemployment level. As already indicated, their general finding that payment for not working lessens incentives to find new work is unassailable, but how important this effect is remains in doubt. After a careful review of the literature, Daniel Hamermesh concluded that if

9. In the 1970s, emergency bills extended the duration of benefits to as much as 65 weeks.

10. *Employment and Training Report of the President, 1977,* p. 270. Not all the increases were due to automatic adjustments in payments.

11. Hamermesh, *Jobless Pay and the Economy,* pp. 60-64.

the unemployment rate were 4 percent in the absence of the unemployment insurance system, the presence of the system raises the rate to about 4.5 percent. Other investigators put the effect at slightly under this amount.[12] Contrary to popular impression, however, this outcome cannot be attributed to the rise in benefit rate levels; since 1956, the years when the level of unemployment in high employment periods rose markedly, the ratio of average unemployment benefits to average weekly earnings only increased by 2.7 percentage points. Essentially the same holds for the lengthening in the period unemployment benefits can be received which now stands at 26 weeks in most states and 39 weeks in a few others; extensions beyond 39 weeks have been permitted but only on a temporary basis and apply to periods of recession rather than to periods of high employment. Even assuming that the longer duration of benefits has served to increase the unemployment level in periods of high employment, it is important to consider whether lengthening search times for locating new and presumably "better" jobs do not carry important benefits for workers, employers and the general public. While some investigators have concluded that longer benefits to individuals have led to higher subsequent earnings when employed, others are skeptical whether the relationship can be quantified.[13] All that can be safely concluded is that the benefits of longer job search offset some portion, conceivably all, of the adverse effects of the system on job seeking behavior.

The main adverse effects of the system on unemployment in high employment environments can be traced to the broadening coverage of the law, first in 1954, when Congress extended the size of covered employers to those with four or

---

12. Ibid., p. 52. See also, Arnold Katz, ed., "The Economics of Unemployment Insurance: A Symposium," *Industrial and Labor Relations Review* (July 1977).

13. Katz, ed., *Economics of Unemployment Insurance,* pp. 433-434.

more employees for 20 weeks a year, then in 1970, to covered employers of one or more employees for 20 weeks a year as well as to most nonprofit organizations and finally in 1976, to almost all of the remaining nonprofit organizations and even some agricultural workers and household domestics. Today, the federal-state unemployment compensation system covers over 95 percent of the country's employed wage and salary employees.

The result has been that many lower skilled workers in relatively unstable jobs are now eligible for unemployment benefits. As a consequence, so it is argued, more persons with unstable job patterns (i.e., who are jobless prone) have entered the labor force and thereby pushed up the unemployment rate. This again raises the vexatious question of the hitherto "discouraged workers" who become encouraged during periods of strong business expansion to seek paying jobs. The fact that many such workers become job holders and job seekers in such periods is clear enough, but whether the prospect of unemployment benefits plays an important part in their behavior is not. Lacking any evidence to the contrary, it seems likely that other and more immediate incentives such as next month's pay check play a far more significant role.

There is one aspect of the matter, however, which warrants special attention, namely the tendency of the unemployment insurance system to promote greater seasonal, and possibly even greater cyclical, instability in employment and output. This follows from the fact that both workers and employers can, at least to some extent, adapt their work behavior and production schedules to take advantage of the system's benefit provisions. Estimates of this effect are, however, subject to innumerable qualifications. On the assumption of an unemployment rate of 4 percent, Hamermesh estimated that this feature of the system has increased the overall rate by about .075 percentage points. If firms were taxed exactly in proportion to their relative unemployment level (i.e., if the experience rating system were perfect), no increase from this source would occur.[14]

Summing up, neither systematic research investigations nor recent experience support the view that the unemployment insurance system has significantly raised the country's unemployment level in high employment periods. Any pronouncements or findings to the contrary call for most cautious treatment or as concluded in a recent symposium on the subject:

> The apparently strong empirical evidence reported here that UI increases unemployment must be weighed against the many pitfalls and still unresolved conceptual issues encountered in measuring UI total benefits.[15]

As regards the effect of specific features of the unemployment insurance system on unemployment, some further strengthening of the experience rating basis of taxing employers in the direction just noted and a general tightening of the work test requirements in a number of the states would seem in order. Similarly, any marked rise in high-employment periods in the present benefit-to-wage ratio would seem imprudent. On the other hand, such sweeping proposals as making unemployment benefits subject to tax or shifting the basis for experience rating from the firm to the individual would not be warranted. Not only would such moves be highly questionable on general economic and social grounds, but also when viewed in more narrow terms their contribution to lowering the unemployment rate would most likely prove insignificant.

---

14. Hamermesh, *Jobless Pay and the Economy,* p. 71.

15. Katz, ed., *Economics of Unemployment Insurance,* p. 437.

Income Support Programs

The effects on the unemployment rate of income support programs on behalf of the nation's poor are even more difficult to pin down than the employment effects of the unemployment insurance system. There are presently over 40 programs which provide such supports. Broadly defined, aid to the poor should include social insurance and medicare, since they provide important benefits to low income groups, but attention here is limited to welfare or means-tested programs.[16]

The current debate over the nation's welfare programs centers largely on the aid to families with dependent children program (AFDC), although the food stamps and medicaid programs have also been receiving increasing attention. AFDC rolls have swelled dramatically since the early 1960s; between 1965 and 1975, for example, total benefit costs rose five times and the number of recipients two and a half times. In July 1976, there were 11 million recipients of whom only about 5.5 percent fell in the unemployed-father category.[17] In more recent years, however, there has been relatively little growth in the welfare rolls.

Three factors were primarily responsible for this increase: the number of families with children headed by women rose sharply, standards of eligibility were loosened, and the proportion of those eligible claiming payments more than doubled. In fiscal 1977, total expenditures on AFDC came to about $10 billion of which a little over half was provided by the federal government and the balance by state and local governments. Since it is highly probable that the level of

---

16. In fiscal 1976 social insurance benefits including unemployment compensation constituted over 50 percent of total income after taxes and transfers of the lowest quintile of the income distribution. Joseph Pechman, ed., *Setting National Priorities: The 1978 Budget* (Washington: Brookings Institution, 1977), p. 252.

17. Ibid., p. 256.

AFDC benefits will be raised still higher in the years ahead and that its coverage will be extended to include even more working persons on low incomes, the question of the effects of this massive program on the unemployment rate is of critical importance.

While a number of aspects of this issue remain unclear, the evidence on certain points is quite firm. First, a substantial proportion (probably over 60 percent) of individuals officially defined as poor, are incapable of working, 44 percent being children, 11 percent aged, and 5 percent nonaged adults; beyond this is an additional percentage accounted for by women with very young children.[18]

Second, poor people capable of working are prepared to work where there is some tangible gain involved and, in the case of welfare mothers, where minimum family needs can be met. Even under the existing welfare system, about 30 percent of the families leave AFDC within a year and 60 percent within three years.[19] In fact, 22 percent of the heads of poor families were found to have worked at least part time and 13 percent full time during the year in fiscal 1978. Moreover, even the proportion of working mothers on welfare who were in the labor force rose from 19 percent in 1961 to 28 percent in 1973. Several controlled experiments in New Jersey and elsewhere have shown that work done by male heads of households would only be reduced by about 5 to 10 percent with the introduction of cash welfare benefits. The reduction for wives and teenagers, however, two groups that are heavily represented among the structurally unemployed, would be considerably greater.[20]

---

18. Ibid., p. 258.

19. Sar A. Levitan, Martin Rein, and David Marwick, *Work and Welfare Go Together* (Baltimore: Johns Hopkins Press, 1973), p. 50.

20. Pechman, ed., *Setting National Priorities: The 1978 Budget,* pp. 258-259.

Third, the present structure of welfare aid in this country still discourages recipients of such aid from taking work. Since 1969 the states have been required to exempt earnings of $30 per month plus one-third of all additional income and work expenses in determining an AFDC family's needs. This leaves little incentive to seek earnings from work as a means of supplementing income from welfare, especially since such earnings are likely to be subject to Social Security tax, federal income tax and possibly state income tax, in addition to the possibility of disqualifying the recipient for any Medicaid benefits whatsoever. Analysis of preliminary data shows that a typical AFDC recipient who accepts a public service employment job, for example, is subject to a 61 percent benefit reduction rate, meaning that after taking account of the reduction in AFDC, food stamps, and child care payments that result from taking one of these jobs, the recipient stands to increase his or her family income by only 39 percent over what would have been received in transfer payments. A major purpose behind the Administration's current proposals to establish a national income guarantee plan is to reduce these overlapping features of the present welfare system and, as a consequence, increase the incentive for recipients to seek work.

Those advocating that all able-bodied persons on welfare take jobs are faced with a formidable dilemma: any voluntary program, to be successful, would require relatively high and therefore very costly wages, while any involuntary program would entail an excessive degree of coercion. A middle road requiring all applicants for AFDC to register in the Work Incentive Program (WIN) has been followed since 1967. Those considered employable were ordered to be ready to go to work or, if no jobs were available, to take training to qualify for later jobs. Initially, emphasis was placed on the training element, but especially since 1971 the focus has been on the job placement provision. Helped by the general up-

swing in business and, to a limited extent, by the more intensive effort to increase job placements, the number of full
time jobs obtained by WIN registrants rose from about
170,000 in fiscal 1975 to nearly 300,000 in fiscal 1976; the
total fell to a little over 250,000 by fiscal 1978.[21]

Critics of the present work and training requirement fall
into two camps. There are those who argue that the greatest
possible emphasis should be placed on voluntary responses
of welfare recipients. This would entail providing them with
a wide range of job and training opportunities in both the
private and public sector at prevailing market wages, opportunities that would be geared to the recipients' long term
career needs and particular capacities. Estimates of the
number of jobs that would be needed to provide work for
every able-bodied person range from 2.5 to 5 million, depending on the wage rate and comprehensiveness of the
coverage.[22] The distinctive feature of this group's view is not
so much the large number of jobs that would be required but
the kinds of jobs and the levels of remuneration that would
be entailed since the terms of employment would have to be
sufficiently favorable to keep the program on a voluntary
response basis.

At the other extreme are those who argue that every
welfare recipient capable of working should be required to
take a job or enter a training program even on terms that
may be considered unacceptable to the individuals involved.

---

21. Since March 1976, AFDC applicants have been required to register at their state
employment service office or (in the case of two states) a similar office, instead of their
local welfare agency. This has had the effect of giving them more direct access to job openings. *Employment and Training Report of the President, 1977,* p. 58.See also the Work Incentive Program 9th Annual Report to the Congress, *WIN: 1968-1978* (U.S. Departments
of Labor and Health, Education and Welfare, 1979; processed).

22. Joint Economic Committee, Subcommittee on Fiscal Policy, *JOIN: A Jobs and Income
Program for American Families,* Studies in Public Welfare, Paper No. 19 (Washington:
Government Printing Office, 1974), p. 60.

They too emphasize the importance of getting people off welfare and into work or training, but they draw the line at providing opportunities that would attract AFDC recipients on a purely voluntary basis. This, it is felt, would entail enormous expense, put people into jobs for which they are not qualified, and in all likelihood lead to a dangerous expansion in the role of government. The key difference in the two views comes in the degree of coercion that would be involved.

The issues raised in this controversy give no promise of being resolved in the near future, but there is a strong likelihood that a middle-road approach will finally emerge if for no other reason than that the practical difficulties of adhering to either of the extreme positions would be enormous. Such an approach would aim at providing work opportunities for welfare recipients at whatever levels they are qualified for and, in the case of those who refuse the opportunities offered, require entrance into a training or work-training program designed to fit them for regular employment. This would involve a very substantial broadening of the WIN program with far greater emphasis than heretofore on making sure that job opportunities appropriate to the skills and personal situations of employable welfare recipients are in fact present.

Viewed in this light the job and career needs of persons on welfare are essentially no different from those not on welfare who also suffer special difficulties in finding and holding jobs. In both instances, the critical questions to be resolved are the same: where are the job and career openings for which they might qualify and how can they acquire the skills and aptitudes necessary to perform these jobs and to enter some type of career? These two questions, to which the remainder of this study is largely addressed, go to the heart of the structural unemployment problem.

Chapter 6
Discriminatory Employment Barriers

In contrast to wage and related forms of exclusion as well as work disincentives associated with income support programs, discriminatory practices barring certain groups from major lines of work because of their race, sex, age or religion are a key element in explaining the persistence of structural unemployment in periods of general prosperity. In fact, based on certain definitions of the term, discrimination can be viewed as the single most important cause of such unemployment.

The clearest but least important forms of discrimination in the job market consist of explicit and direct bars to employment based on personal attributes wholly unrelated to performance in the particular work involved, such as exclusion of qualified nonwhites from certain lines of factory or office work. A much more significant type of discrimination consists of general institutional bars to employment which limit different groups of the population to certain fields of work, largely excluding them from most others. The latter barrier shows up in statistics on the occupational distribution of nonwhites and of women, the well-known phenomenon of "blacks' jobs" and "women's jobs," but its exact nature is hard to identify. A complete explanation would doubtless take account of a broad range of historical influences including the heritage of the southern plantation system, the development of the family, the country's educational structure, the shift from a rural-agriculture to an urban-factory environment, and the like. Again, the exact extent of this barrier is hard to measure but there is no reason to doubt its pervasiveness and deep-seated character.

Confronted with these two types of limitations, nonwhites and women frequently face but two alternatives in a given labor market: either accept work in the narrowly defined lines that by longstanding custom have come to be designated for them, or subsist on income from unemployment insurance, welfare or a variety of borderline and even illicit activities. In tightly constricted environments of this sort, confirming attitude and behavior patterns are likely to spread, affecting broader groups of workers, employers and members of the general public. As a result, a virtually impregnable set of barriers may emerge, cutting off many nonwhite and women workers from the broader labor market, and inducing either relatively high unemployment rates or increased dropout rates from the labor force.

Despite these adverse circumstances, important progress has been made since the early 1940s in opening up career opportunities for nonwhites and women. The tight labor markets associated with World War II provided a powerful thrust in this direction. Later, with the long upswing of the 1960s, both groups began to enter career lines that had been previously closed to them. Fewer than one out of five nonwhites worked in white-collar occupations in 1964 but by 1974 about one in three were in these jobs. During this period there was a significant drop in the proportion of nonwhites in service occupations, particularly the private household category. Within the blue-collar field, there was a substantial shift among such workers from the unskilled into the operative and craft trades during this same period (see table 6-1).

Table 6-1
Employment by Occupation Group and Race, 1964 and 1974
(Percent distribution)

| | 1964 | | 1974 | |
Occupation group	White	Negro and other races	White	Negro and other races
Total: Number (thousands)......	61,922	7,383	76,620	9,316
Percent.................	100.0	100.0	100.0	100.0
White-collar workers...........	47.6	6.8	50.6	32.0
Professional and technical.....	13.0	6.8	14.8	10.4
Managers and administrators,				
except farm...............	11.7	2.6	11.2	4.1
Sales workers...............	6.6	1.7	6.8	2.3
Clerical workers..............	16.3	7.7	17.8	15.2
Blue-collar workers.............	36.1	40.6	33.9	40.2
Craft and kindred...........	13.7	7.1	13.3	9.4
Operatives..................	18.4	20.5	15.5	21.9
Nonfarm laborers...........	4.1	13.0	4.6	8.9
Service workers...............	10.5	32.3	12.0	25.1
Farmworkers..................	5.8	8.4	3.6	2.7

Source: Manpower Report of the President, 1975, p. 34.

Note: The data for 1974 are not strictly comparable with those of 1964 as a result of changes in the classification of occupations to accord with the 1970 Census. Detail may not add to totals because of rounding.

Important as these gains are, nonwhites remain seriously underrepresented in the higher status occupations. In 1974, about 15 percent of white workers were in the professional category and 11 percent in the managerial and administrative category as against only 10 percent and 4 percent respectively of nonwhite workers (see table 6-1).

While nonwhites were scoring these relatively modest gains, women during this period achieved even fewer. Between 1947 and 1976 the proportion of women in the nation's civilian labor force rose from about 17 percent to 40 percent but their concentration in the "feminine" jobs of secretaries and typists, retail clerks, bookkeepers, teachers and waitresses remained nearly as great as before.[1] Women have made some headway in breaking into such professions as accounting, where they constitute about 24 percent of the total, but still make up only miniscule proportions of such professional groups as physicians and lawyers.

During the 1970s there was some further improvement in the occupational status of nonwhites and women, particularly if the comparisons are limited to relatively prosperous years when the unemployment rate stood at 6 percent or less. Between 1969 and 1978, for example, the proportion of nonwhites (black and other) in the professional and technical category rose from 8.3 to 11.7 percent while the proportion in the managers and administrators category rose from 2.5 to 4.8 percent. Similarly, the proportion of women in the former category rose from 13.8 to 15.6 percent and in the latter category from 4.3 to 6.1 percent over this same period. Similar shifts, though less clearcut, occurred in such blue-collar categories as craft and kindred workers.[2] These gains were especially noteworthy since, in relation to 1969, labor market conditions in 1978 were comparatively unfavorable. Again, however, the improvements did not alter the occupational distribution in favor of these groups in any fundamental way.

The fact that many nonwhites and women are effectively cut off from a wide range of employment opportunities because of their race and sex leads directly to more structural unemployment. Once employed, these workers are generally not allowed to compete for any openings other than in their restricted zones of work, even though many vacancies may have developed in other fields. The indirect, long term effects, however, are far more serious. Workers subject to

---

1. *Manpower Report of the President, 1975* (Washington: Government Printing Office, 1976), p. 32.

2. *Employment and Training Report of the President, 1979,* pp. 261 and 263.

labor market discrimination see little to be gained from acquiring advanced skills if there is hardly any probability of their being used. Improved work habits, closer attention on the job, more readiness to cooperate with others—these are attributes which are associated with stable work histories and a reasonable chance for career advancement; they have much less, if any, meaning where jobs are highly unstable and career progression very unlikely. In these circumstances, employer attitudes towards such workers tend to become increasingly negative so that not even the first steps towards better training and improved job performance are likely to be taken. The attitudes of more experienced workers and even the general public become more negative and the circle of negative expectations and work-resistant practices is thereby made complete.

Reducing Discriminatory Barriers

The main effort to break through these barriers by legal means and open a wider range of job opportunities to the disadvantaged stems from the Civil Rights Act of 1964. Under Title VII of this law, a five-member Equal Employment Opportunity Commission (EEOC) has the responsibility of assuring that hiring, promotion and firing are on the basis of ability and qualifications without regard to race, color, religious belief, sex or national origin. The main work of the Commission has consisted of investigating complaints of discrimination on a case-by-case basis and encouraging compliance through informal conciliation procedures. In the 31 states with Fair Employment Practices Commissions, EEOC must defer action for 60 days until the state or local unit has shown an inability to resolve the complaint. Prior to 1972, legal action to implement the terms of Title VII could only be brought by private parties or by the Justice Department, an especially expensive and formidable procedure from the viewpoint of lower paid workers. An important change occurred in that year when Congress authorized EEOC to bring civil suits on its own motion. Fear of legal action and the possibility of costly settlements has induced more willingness among employers to agree to voluntary settlements.

The trend was accelerated when EEOC became more active in filing civil court class action cases. A significant turning point occurred in 1973 when American Telephone and Telegraph signed a consent decree providing $15 million in restitution and back pay for several classes of female employees and a $23 million promotion package for women and minorities.[3] Two other actions were: (1) the 1974 consent decree entered into by nine major steel companies and the United Steelworkers granting 40,000 minority and women workers $30.9 million in back pay and establishing goals and timetables to increase the number of women and minority workers in areas in which they had been underrepresented;[4] (2) the 1978 settlement agreed to by General Electric which provided $29.4 million in benefits to women and minority workers plus $3 million to improve affirmative action plans.[5]

The Commission's impact on employment practices also increased as it developed more precise definitions and criteria in passing on discrimination cases. Thus, an employer was entitled to set tests or other objective standards for hiring but these must be related to job performance and not serve merely as a discriminatory screening device. Employers subject to Title VII are now prohibited from recruiting through their current employees or through the

---

3. In 1978, the Supreme Court left standing a lower court decision upholding this decree, thereby indicating support for affirmative action programs that remedy past discrimination in employment even when they conflict with established union seniority systems. *New York Times,* July 4, 1978.

4. Levitan, Mangum, and Marshall, *Human Resources and Labor Markets,* p. 454.

5. *New York Times,* June 16, 1978.

union office if they get few black applicants and the racial composition of their workforce differs significantly from that of the community.[6] The courts have moved, though with less success, to establish similar criteria with respect to union participation in hiring and recruitment procedures, notably in the building trades.

The other main legal device for putting job opportunities on a nondiscriminatory basis is based on Executive Order 11246 which was issued by President Johnson and which President Nixon allowed to remain in effect. The Executive Order is administered by the Department of Labor's Office of Federal Contract Compliance (OFCC). The order covers all employers who have federal contracts and includes companies with an estimated employment of 40 million persons, about two-fifths of the labor force. It not only forbids contractors to discriminate on the basis of race, creed, color, sex, or national origin, but also requires that they take "affirmative action" to guarantee equal access.

Under this requirement, companies must make an analysis of all major job classifications and provide an explanation for any underutilization of minorities; they must further set specific goals to remedy any identified shortcomings and supply relevant data to the appropriate government organizations on racial-occupational categories, racial backgrounds of job applicants, job progression charts and seniority rosters. Affirmative action under Executive Order 11246 may in given cases require still further steps on the part of companies to increase and upgrade minority employment: recruiting visits to secondary schools with high black enrollment; advertising for employees in black community newspapers; and special training courses for the transfer and upgrading of black employees into all-white departments. In

---

6. See symposium, "Employment Discrimination and Title VII of the Civil Rights Act of 1964," *Harvard Law Review* (March 1971), p. 1114 ff.

the case of the construction industry, minority employment goals, as opposed to quotas, have been set for individual crafts in some cities in accordance with the "Philadelphia Plan" concept (discussed below). It should be noted that Executive Order 11246, unlike Title VII, contains stiff sanctions including cancellation, termination, suspension of contracts and "blacklisting" of noncomplying companies.[7]

The predominant view among impartial investigators is that, while significant in individual cases, these two legal devices have as yet had little observable impact on general hiring and employment practices. Stress is laid on the fact that the Justice Department's Civil Rights Division has a very limited staff assigned to this area of work, that the focus of both the EEOC and OFCC is still on case-by-case dealings with individual (usually large) companies and chiefly on mere appeals for voluntary cooperation.

In the case of EEOC, Congress has rejected efforts to amend Title VII so that it would have the power to issue cease-and-desist orders, thereby severely undercutting its activities. While OFCC on the other hand has sanction powers, it has invoked them but rarely; moreover, its executive orders refer only to government contractors and do not directy affect unions even in situations where they are the major or exclusive sources of labor.

Critics have put greatest emphasis on the need for drastic administrative reforms. In late 1977, EEOC had a backlog of 130,000 unsettled cases and two years were required to settle the average case. Since its inception in 1965, the agency has had seven chairmen, three in the three years ending in 1977. OFCC also appears to have lacked any clear direction. Enforcement procedures have been particularly weak, with only fifteen noncomplying employers barred from getting

---

7. See Gordon F. Bloom and Herbert R. Northrup, *Economics of Labor Relations,* pp. 705-714.

more federal contracts in twelve years in the pre-1977 period. It is also charged that while these two agencies are mainly responsible for the government's antidiscrimination efforts, there are in fact twenty-five separate agencies, each with its own rules and procedures, operating in this field. In the words of a 1976 report of the House Labor Committee's Subcommittee on Equal Opportunities:

> Our findings indicate a weak, uncoordinated and largely ineffective enforcement effort on the part of those agencies charged with preventing employment discrimination.[8]

Since 1977, a determined effort has been made to reduce the backlog of cases at EEOC and to strengthen the enforcement procedures of OFCC, but much work remains to be done.

Antidiscrimination Policies and Structural Unemployment

While overhaul of the government's administrative machinery in this field is clearly called for, the question at issue here is whether even the most efficiently run program would make a major contribution to reducing structural unemployment within the foreseeable future. In terms of providing a general framework for effective action, the answer is definitely in the affirmative, but in terms of specific lines of action, the answer appears to be quite otherwise. Except where explicit forms of discrimination are involved, the issues are not clearcut enough to be handled by legal means. In attempting to apply uniform antidiscrimination requirements to widely diverse work situations, the limits where the rights and interest of injured groups also become involved are soon reached. Other factors having to do with the general level of employment, productivity differences, and the like have a more direct bearing on the

8. *Wall Street Journal,* August 26, 1977.

nature and extent of structural unemployment. Unless these direct factors can be substantially altered, attempts to reduce such unemployment by antidiscrimination directives are almost bound to fail.

What, then, are the conditions that would have to be met if an antidiscrimination program for dealing with structural unemployment were to be successful? First, as already indicated, labor markets would have to be generally tight. As long as there is an overall slack in employment that affects even "fully qualified, fully acceptable" workers, those viewed as less qualified are apt to continue to be largely blocked from employment.

Second, where jobs are to be made available to workers who are viewed as being less qualified, certain economic incentives and perhaps penalties will be required. This may entail subsidies and tax adjustments to induce employers, unions or particular worker groups to assume the added costs. Efforts to promote job entry by quota, however, will almost surely encounter severe resistance, so chief emphasis will still need to be placed on voluntary acceptance by the parties involved.

Third, explicit provision will be needed to insure that the productivity of such workers is brought up to the levels normally required of new hires. While it is clear that many of the factors determining job performance, such as one's neighborhood environment, quality of educational preparation, and type of previous skill training, may themselves be the product of discrimination, it is equally clear that directing employers to take on less productive workers without explicit recognition of the extra costs involved can hardly prove successful. Rather, the focus of public policy should be on giving discriminated workers as much opportunity to increase their productive efficiency as workers generally, but not to guarantee job entry regardless of performance considerations.

Fourth, extensive governmental effort along a variety of related lines aimed at reducing other barriers to employment will be required if any real progress is to be made against discrimination in labor markets. In some communities, particularly in large metropolitan areas, a major overhaul in transportation facilities may be necessary; in some, extensive changes in housing patterns; in others, substantial infusions of capital in potential growth fields accessible to hard-to-employ groups; in still others, sustained campaigns to raise the quality of educational opportunities available to young people from disadvantaged families. Unless there is public acceptance of the need for strong (and costly!) actions along these lines, legal restrictions on discriminatory employment practices designed to reduce structural unemployment will prove largely fruitless.

Hiring Goals, Seniority and Apprentice Programs

The difficulties besetting present programs become clear when attention centers on particular issues, three of which will be noted here. The first is the use of specific goals and timetables as a means of raising the proportion of blacks or other disadvantaged groups in higher skilled occupations. This has remained a highly controversial issue ever since 1967 when the Department of Labor's Office of Federal Contract Compliance sought to require building contractors in Philadelphia to commit themselves to specific goals of minority manpower utilization.

Rather than impose specific quotas, the government soon made clear that it merely required good faith effort on the contractors' part to meet their commitment to attain certain goals.[9] Similar efforts have been made in Chicago, Seattle

9. This was the federal district court's view of the Philadelphia Plan; see Contractors Association of Eastern Pennsylvania v. Shultz, District Court, Eastern Pennsylvania (1970); the Supreme Court refused to review this case.

and some twenty other cities, though with greater emphasis on voluntary agreements between union, contractor and minority group representatives. Even in the relatively prosperous pre-1974 years, however, a survey of 31 of 70 government-approved plans showed that less than a third of the local unions had met their goals. Given continued sluggish conditions in construction, it is doubtful that this record has been improved subsequently.

However laudable their objectives, progress under affirmative action plans will necessarily be painfully slow except under conditions of extremely tight labor supplies. In looser supply situations, workers who long since achieved journeyman or related skill status will quite understandably insist on filling whatever openings may occur. To do otherwise would mean, at least in the short run, supplanting the more experienced and presumably more skilled with the less experienced and the less skilled. Such bald displays of reverse discrimination could hardly provide a solid basis for public policy.

As to the strictly legal issues involved, much confusion exists over how far private parties or the government can go in this direction without causing reverse bias prohibited by the 1964 Civil Rights Act or by the guarantees of equal protection and due process provided by the Constitution. Under recent rulings of the Supreme Court the principle that affirmative action plans are legal is now quite firmly established. True, in the 1978 Alan Bakke case, the Court held by a 5 to 4 vote that it was illegal for the University of California at Davis to reserve 16 of the 100 places in its medical school class for minorities, but in the 1979 Brian Weber case the Court, by a 5 to 2 vote, held that a voluntary affirmative action plan reserving half the slots in a skilled-craft training program at the Kaiser Aluminum and Chemical Corporation was legal. Moreover, in the 1980 Fullilove case the Court, by a 6 to 3 vote, upheld the constitutionality of Congressional legislation establishing a federal public works program in which 10 percent of spending was reserved for minority contractors.[10] Whether the Supreme Court will follow the same reasoning embodied in the Weber and Fullilove decisions with respect to questions of hiring, layoffs and promotion remains unclear, but the widespread impact on affirmative action policies of these two decisions will doubtless be marked.

Even if the legal basis of such policies becomes firmly established, their effectiveness as a means for reducing structural unemployment would remain in doubt. Much would depend on how much emphasis is placed on specific restrictions and directives as against more positive, voluntary actions. If it is concluded that existing job holders will have to lose their positions to make way for minority workers, little observable effect can be expected. If, on the other hand, emphasis is placed on making sure that minority workers can qualify for any future openings that might occur, a significant impact on the structural unemployment problem might well occur. To the extent that legislation provides the general framework within which employers, unions and local communities work out their employment problems, antidiscrimination laws are essential to effective action against structural unemployment, but little contribution can be expected if it means that existing job holders will be displaced.

A second issue leading to essentially the same result involves restructuring seniority systems to eliminate discriminatory practices. In many firms, each department has its own seniority roster and since entry to departments with the better jobs was previously allocated along racial and

---

10. Regents of the University of California v. Bakke, 438 U.S. 298 (1978); Steelworkers Union v. Weber, 443 U.S. 193; Fullilove v. Klutznick, Secretary of Commerce, No. 78-1007 (July 2, 1980).

sex lines, it becomes critically important whether departmental seniority will be allowed to continue. This, however, is just the first phase in what is frequently an extremely complicated restructuring process. If a firm or a firm and union are required to shift to a plant-wide seniority system, should provision be made for redressing past patterns of discrimination? It could well be argued that simply permitting previously excluded workers to gain places, presumably near the bottom, in a broadened seniority system would not put them on an equal footing in competing for available jobs; yet how far should the courts go in ordering firms to give preference to these workers over other more experienced and, at least in an immediate sense, more qualified workers?

Thus far the courts have tried to follow a middle path through this labyrinth. Thus, they have generally struck down specific features of a seniority system that have the effect of excluding particular groups from jobs because of race or sex, e.g., unnecessarily long training periods or reductions in wages as a condition for transfers.[11] On the other hand the courts have held that no penalties can be imposed for discriminatory acts committed before the Civil Rights Act of 1964. In what may prove to be a landmark decision, the U.S. Supreme Court recently ruled that employees locked into inferior positions because of pre-Act discriminatory seniority provisions could get no relief, but that for employees hired after the Act, complete relief, including retroactive seniority as far back as the effective date of the Act, is available. The Court based this finding on Section 703(h) of Title VII which it interpreted as meaning that Congress did not intend to make it illegal for employees with vested seniority rights to

---

11. U.S. v. United Paper Makers, Local 189, 71 LRRM 2005 (1968) and Hicks v. Crown Zellerback Corp., 69 LRRM 2005 (1968).

continue to exercise those rights, even at the expense of pre-Act discriminatees.[12]

However the question of segregated seniority rosters is approached, it is evident that the process of resolving the respective claims involved can only come slowly. No formula is at hand for cutting through the various interests at stake in any sweeping manner; a laborious and probably often frustrating case-by-case approach seems inescapable. To make this a major strategy for coping with structural unemployment, therefore, would not seem promising.

A third issue to be considered is the development of broader apprenticeship programs and (quite the opposite consideration) a general attempt to deal with the "over-credential" problem in employer hiring and promotion procedures. Both aspects of this issue bear on the role of education and training in structural unemployment, the subject of the next section of this study. Here, attention is limited to any discriminatory elements that may be involved.

Apprenticeship programs, whereby trainees work with experienced journeymen for a stated period at lower wages while they acquire the necessary "outside" training, have largely been confined to construction, metal trades, printing and such occupations as meat cutters and telephone linemen and servicemen. As shown in table 6-2, the total number of apprentices registered under government sponsorship has come to a little under 300,000 in recent years as against about 160,000 in the mid-1950s. While numerically still unimportant, apprenticeship training provides a clear-cut means for inexperienced workers with limited education to gain access

---

12. International Brotherhood of Teamsters v. United States, U.S. Supreme Court, Nos. 75-636 and 75-672, May 31, 1977. Section 703(h) reads in part: ". . . it shall not be an unlawful employment practice for an employer to apply different standards of compensation, or different terms, conditions, or privileges of employment pursuant to a bona fide seniority . . . system, provided that such differences are not the result of an intention to discriminate because of race . . . or national origin. . . ."

to higher skilled, better paying jobs. Some progress has been made in achieving greater minority worker participation in such programs; according to the 1960 census, nonwhites accounted for only 2.5 percent of the total, but by 1975 they made up about 17 percent. Women remained but a tiny portion, approximately 2 percent of the total.[13]

Table 6-2
Training Status of Registered Apprentices, Selected Years, 1955-75

	(in thousands)
1955	159
1960	172
1965	171
1970	270
1973*	251
1975	285
1977	362

Source: Employment and Training Report of the President, 1977, Table F-14, p. 274, and 1979, pp. 56-57.
*New nationwide data system introduced January 1, 1973.

The reasons for the limited progress are clear enough: in slack labor markets particularly, neither employers nor existing journeyman groups are likely to be willing to extend apprenticeship programs to new, hitherto excluded, categories of workers. Nor, given the institutional limitations affecting their preparation and attitudes, are minority applicants and women likely to have the qualifications for entering such programs, assuming they even know of their existence. A sustained government effort on both fronts could yield significant results if job prospects become more favorable.

A feature of apprentice and less formal recruitment procedures that has become the center of much controversy is

13. Employment and Training Report of the President, 1977, pp. 67-68.

whether entrance or hiring qualifications in certain career lines are kept unnecessarily high, with the effect of 'excluding most minority and women applicants. Some apprentice plans require as much as six years of training before journeyman status is achieved, considerably longer than could conceivably be justified on grounds of skill acquisition. In certain crafts where belonging to a union is a prerequisite for entering a trade, training requirements are set in such a way that membership is largely limited to relatives or personal friends of existing members. Employers sometimes also establish educational or intelligence test requirements which largely rule out minority or women applicants for certain jobs. Title VII of the Civil Rights Act of 1964 has gone a long way toward prohibiting such barriers to job openings. Whether more aggressive government action would have a significantly greater impact is debatable. In the 1971 Griggs case, the Supreme Court ruled that Title VII "proscribes not only overt discrimination but also practices that are fair in form, but discriminatory in action."[14] Thus, pre-employment tests that were not job related were ruled illegal, since they were likely to exclude minority applicants; also tests were barred that operaate to disqualify nonwhite applicants at a substantially higher rate than white applicants or tests relating to a job formerly filled only by white employees as a matter of company policy.

This aspect of employer and union employment practices is crucially important in any broad effort to reduce labor market discrimination, but whether it could ever serve as a major strategy in reducing structural unemployment is doubtful. Except in extreme cases it is frequently very difficult to show that failure to hire particular workers was not based on differences in experience, ability or some other "objective" hiring criterion. In view of the legal complex-

---

14. Griggs v. Duke Power Company, U.S. Supreme Court, No. 124, March 9, 1971.

ities and pitfalls which have come to surround pre-employment testing since the Civil Rights Act, many firms have moved away from using formal test procedures altogether. Whether legal limitations on such procedures could be applied in such a way as to have an observable impact on structural unemployment is questionable. In any event, the overcredentialing problem tends to disappear as expansions broaden and labor supplies become tighter.

Chapter 7
Strengthening Educational Opportunities

In any discussion of barriers to employment confronting certain groups in the working population, the role of public education must be given central attention. It falls to the country's elementary and secondary schools to provide the basic skills that underlie all lines of work; since many workers among the structurally unemployed do not possess the essential skills needed to meet minimum employable standards, the country's school system must play a central role in any national effort to overcome their deficiencies. The following discussion is addressed to the federal government's part in such an undertaking.

Strengthening Educational Opportunities

When attention was first drawn in the 1960s to the paradox of high unemployment in periods of prosperity and the persistence of poverty in an affluent society, the idea gained wide currency that if basic education programs could be fashioned to the particular needs of potentially hard-to-employ groups, the way would subsequently open to their getting more and better work opportunities. This was in line with the approach pursued by immigrant groups in earlier decades to gain entry into the mainstream of American economic life and it fitted well into the country's tradition of education for all. Strong efforts were accordingly made during the decade of the 1960s to develop special educational programs which would widen existing and future job opportunities of the disadvantaged among youth, women, blacks and nonblack minorities.

These special efforts grew out of the much more inclusive educational systems that had been developed for the public at large. While bearing many of the same characteristics, the programs designed on behalf of disadvantaged groups were heavily weighted on the side of career preparation or re-entry: acquisition of essential comprehension-communication abilities, development of at least some rudimentary work skills, and personal help in discovering and pursuing career interests. Special emphasis was placed on providing the extra professional and personal attention required to help these groups overcome the educational and related barriers associated with their disadvantaged backgrounds.

The high optimism with which this aspect of the War on Poverty was undertaken in the early 1960s gave way to an equally deep pessimism in the early 1970s.[1] Here again, the disappointment felt towards these special programs for the disadvantaged was paralleled by a disillusionment with educational programs generally. While more dramatic and tragic in its implications, the inability to deal effectively with the educational deficiencies of the disadvantaged was matched by a mounting criticism of the nation's entire educational

---

1. The change in viewpoint regarding education was first spelled out in James Coleman et al., *Equality of Educational Opportunity* (Washington: Government Printing Office, 1966). A most influential study in the same vein was Christopher Jencks et al., *Inequality: A Reassessment of the Effect of Family and Schooling in America* (New York: Basic Books, 1972). For an early critique of this viewpoint, see Charles S. Benson (director), *Final Report to the Senate Select Committee on School District Finance*, Vol. 1 (Sacramento, CA: The Committee, 1972, processed). The most serious weakness of the Coleman Report, one that Coleman himself has recognized, is that limitations of data obliged his group to consider only physical resource differences among schools and not such things as how teachers organize their classrooms.

structure and practices—its costs, methods and even overall direction.

As for governmental efforts aimed at improving the cognitive skills of disadvantaged students, particularly those in inner-city ghettos, the major findings of investigators during the late 1960s and early 1970s, findings which continue to have considerable influence today, were set forth by one scholar in the following terms:

> The most comprehensive review of the literature on this subject concludes that [compensatory] education programs—on the average—have not been successful in improving the relative performance of disadvantaged students, and studies of educational effectiveness offer little basis for optimism that the schools can be used to create such impacts.[2]

Similarly with respect to special efforts to lengthen the schooling period of disadvantaged students, the same scholar concluded:

> To summarize, the strategy of alleviating poverty through programs that encourage disadvantaged persons to obtain more schooling seems to have been characterized by two shortcomings. First, it does not appear that the programs were very successful in raising educational attainments [i.e., lengthening the schooling of disadvantaged students]. Second, it does not seem likely that increasing educational attainments of the existing poor would have reduced the poverty class in a society where there are simply an inadequate number of jobs at wages above the poverty level to absorb all job seekers.[3]

---

2. Robert A. Haveman, ed., *A Decade of Federal Antipoverty Programs* (New York: Academic Press, 1977), p. 158, citing Harvey A. Averch et al., *How Effective Is Schooling?* (Englewood Cliffs, NJ: Educational Technology Publications, 1974).

3. Ibid., p. 170.

Promising Approaches

Contrary to the earlier investigations by Coleman and others, a number of recent studies indicate that differences among inner-city schools and, perhaps more significantly, differences among individual classrooms, determine whether disadvantaged students succeed or fail in acquiring fundamental skills. The more important of these studies were conducted by Ronald Edmonds and John Frederickson of Harvard, George Weber, formerly of the Council for Basic Education, and Michael Rutter of the University of London.

Current views about the federal government's Head Start program illustrates this change in outlook. This program was started in 1965 to provide a stimulating learning environment for preschool children from low income families on the assumption they would retain important long term educational benefits from the experience. Following the highly critical Westinghouse-Ohio Report issued in 1969, attitudes toward Head Start changed radically; according to the Report, any cognitive and affective gains from the program largely disappeared by the time children reached second and third grades.

More recent investigations, notably the 1974 HEW study, *Lasting Effects After Preschool,* indicate that the benefits of Head Start have proven much more lasting after all. This study pooled the research efforts of twelve investigators who had independently conducted experimental preschool studies and covered the school careers on a longitudinal basis of participating and nonparticipating students who had reached the ages of 10 to 19 years of age. This relatively long term study concluded that the program did in fact yield long-lasting benefits in that participants were less likely than nonparticipants to require placement in special remedial classes, to be retained in grade, or to score poorly in standardized mathematics achievement tests compared to control groups.[4]

A similar shift in viewpoint, though less clear-cut, has occurred more generally among research scholars who have studied elementary and secondary compensatory educational programs for disadvantaged students. For example, a report to a presidential commission on school finance concluded that where conditions in the school environment are essentially the same for disadvantaged as for nondisadvantaged students, the comparative ratio of progress among the two groups does not appear to be significantly different.[5] This finding is particularly significant in view of the fact that the school environment of disadvantaged students generally falls far short of the school environment enjoyed by students from nondisadvantaged backgrounds. Admitting the limitations of dollar expenditures as a measure of differences in school conditions, it is nonetheless revealing that in a state such as New York, school districts spend on the average more than twice as much per student in elementary and secondary public schools as the average district in nine other states. More important, even after excluding a few of the very highest spending districts, per pupil expenditures within states vary even more widely. Furthermore:

> . . . the districts with the highest expenditure levels in any state tend to be found in the wealthiest suburban areas. Central cities, which on the whole spend well above the statewide average, normally exceed by a slight amount the expenditure levels of the average district in the suburbs. At the bottom of the spectrum are the

---

4. United States Department of Health, Education and Welfare, Consortium for Longitudinal Studies, *Lasting Effects After Preschool* (Washington: Government Printing Office, 1976).

5. Harvey A. Averch et al., "How Effective Is Schooling? A Critical Review and Synthesis of Research Findings," *Final Report to the President's Commission on School Finance* (Santa Monica, CA: Rand Corporation, 1971), pp. 100-108.

school districts in nonmetropolitan areas, which spend considerably less per student that those in urbanized regions.[6]

Where expenditure per student is relatively high in central cities, the result is more a reflection of relatively fewer students than of higher expenditures as such; in metropolitan areas like Boston, New York, Philadelphia, Chicago and San Francisco, public school enrollment as a percentage of total population is about 80 percent of its level in the surrounding suburbs.[7]

A related finding, which is as widely accepted though harder to measure, is that the same educational outcomes would require substantially higher expenditures per pupil in central city districts and certain rural areas than in higher income districts. Inner-city schools, for example, have to spend substantial sums just to protect themselves: vandalism alone cost the New York City school system $3.7 million even in 1971. The buildings in central cities tend to be much older than in many of the more recently developed new suburbs, and costs of maintenance and operation correspondingly higher. Children who require relatively expensive special programs to achieve the same quality standards prevailing elsewhere are often concentrated in central city schools since they need special help to learn what middle class children learn at home; they also require more expensive equipment since they have greater need of vocational and technical training. Thus it has been estimated that, adjusting for the quality factor alone, New York City would have to spend $1,334 per pupil to provide the same schooling that would cost $1,000 in the nearby affluent community of Scarsdale.[8]

6. Robert D. Reischauer et al., *Reforming School Finance* (Washington: The Brookings Institution, 1973), pp. 65-67.

7. Ibid., p. 68.

8. Ibid., p. 64, quoting estimates based on the National Educational Finance Project.

The thrust of these findings is clear: vigorous additional measures need to be taken to overcome the wide gap which is still keeping young people of disadvantaged backgrounds from getting an education that is anywhere near equivalent to the education received by students from more favored backgrounds. The argument that "the poor deserve what they get" is suspect enough when applied to adults; to use it to explain why an inner-city elementary school child should receive a substantially poorer educational opportunity than a child of similar age in a nearby suburb seems patently illogical. If there is genuine concern over the overall cost of education, cutbacks should be confined to the upper income areas when students are least in need of expensive-type programs. Exactly where and how the relative increase in expenditures on low income area programs should be introduced is admittedly unclear, but that the gap in "equivalent" dollar expenditures should be narrowed much further is hardly contestable.

Estimates of the cost of overcoming such disparities vary widely, depending on the assumptions used. The one thing all such estimates have in common is that the dollar totals involved are quite astronomical. Just to bring each state up to the median spending level of all states by means of a flat federal grant of about $500 per student in 1972 would have cost roughly $23 billion annually. To have gone further and removed most intrastate disparities in 1972 would have cost another $8-9 billion annually.[9] If the only groups involved had been disadvantaged students in inner-city districts and certain rural areas, the cost would have been considerably less, but political realities would have made it difficult to limit the grant system in this way. There is no denying that effective action in this direction would place a heavy strain

---

9. Charles L. Schultze et al., *Setting National Priorities: The 1973 Budget* (Washington: The Brookings Institution, 1972), pp. 348 and 351.

on the federal-state-local tax structure or, alternatively, on the allocation of government expenditures to other public needs.

Policy Proposals

Assuming substantial progress is made to equalize educational opportunities along the above lines, what directions of change would most likely contribute to more stable work histories of disadvantaged students in their later careers? The literature is replete with ad hoc insights and proposals for change but there does not appear to be any single strategy commanding general support. The underlying difficulty, as emphasized in the 1966 Coleman Report and repeatedly stressed in subsequent investigations, is that many disadvantaged students come from, and look forward to, environments which destroy any motivation a student might have to progress academically, to move towards a career choice and develop the skills required to implement such a choice. This is simply to say that a person from an unstable, deprived home environment, living in an impoverished, crime-ridden neighborhood, attending an overcrowded, inadequately equipped school, who sees no likelihood of getting a good paying, stable job after finishing his or her education or entering a worthwhile career of any sort, is very apt to be scholastically unmotivated. The astounding fact is how many students from this type of background complete their programs successfully.

At the same time it is important to realize that students from disadvantaged backgrounds vary widely with respect to their educational interests, motivations and capabilities, much more widely than between the disadvantaged and non-disadvantaged considered as two contrasting groups. The same generalization holds for both: there is no single course of study or philosophy of learning which can be said to be most effective (however the latter term may be defined) for either group. The chief difference in practice is that the requisite degree of educational differentiation has been carried considerably further for the nondisadvantaged than the disadvantaged. The former are more likely to have the necessary background to be able to choose among different avenues of study; they have a better chance to translate their study interests into long term careers; and their immediate school environments are more likely to permit or encourage this kind of selective choice and experimentation. Under these conditions, the assumption that individual students can move ahead as far as their motivation and ability will permit is wholly appropriate, but where these conditions do not hold, the assumption makes little or no sense. Again, if the schools are to have any meaningful impact on structural unemployment and related problems of the disadvantaged, the characteristics and conditions of their programs must parallel those available to the nondisadvantaged.

This is the major thrust of the recent report on the country's high schools by the Carnegie Council on Policy Studies in Higher Education. In the words of that report:

> It is clear that many high school students—and junior high school students as well—are getting little out of school, because they simply do not see the relevance to their future lives of what the school is attempting to teach them. We believe that school might become more meaningful to them if there were more options available for combinations of school and work experience.[10]

Given this important caveat, recent investigators have uncovered certain characteristics of compensatory educational programs which appear to explain their relative effectiveness. The theme of their studies is that in a successful compensatory program, the school's principal and teaching

10. *Giving Youth a Better Chance* (San Francisco: Jossey-Bass, 1979), p. 107.

staff have managed to develop a general atmosphere where students have come to accept learning as the focus of their school experience. According to Ronald Edmonds and John Frederickson of Harvard University, the characteristics of successful inner-city schools are:

1. Strong leadership by the principal.
2. Clearly understood teaching objectives.
3. A school climate that is safe, orderly, attractive and serious.
4. High expectations for all students.
5. The use of standardized tests to measure progress and to make plans for what to do next.

As Edmonds, who also is assistant to the New York City Chancellor for instruction in the public schools, acknowledges, these five characteristics could be more effects rather than causes, but he asserts:

> What we are claiming is that these schools as organizations have consistent and observable differences.[11]

This same position was expressed earlier in a Brookings Institution report:

> For the most part these successful compensatory programs featured tightly structured approaches with constant supervision and guidance from a staff that had been trained well and had engaged in considerable planning.[12]

Another major finding of scholars working in this area is that students from disadvantaged backgrounds are in special need of bridging-type relationships between their school ex-

---

11. *New York Times,* December 26, 1979. Roughly similar findings have been reached by a number of other scholars including Richard J. Murnane of Yale, George Weber, formerly of the Council for Basic Education, and Michael Rutter of the University of London.

12. Schultze et al., *Setting National Priorities: The 1973 Budget,* p. 358.

perience on the one hand and their home background, job requirements and community environment on the other. In any given case, one or more of these relationships may be seriously crippling, rendering any meaningful school experience quite impossible. Hence, close working relations will have to be developed between home, school and community to take account of this factor, whether to build on it, alter it in some crucial respect or act to offset its negative impact.

Further, special procedures will have to be devised to link the learning experience of disadvantaged students to different job and career possibilities without cutting them off from the more general aspects of educational preparation. While account will need to be taken of different interests and aptitudes, some direct exposure to work situations will be essential for students from disadvantaged backgrounds and, incidentally, for many nondisadvantaged students as well. Finally, close ties will have to be established between schools and major community institutions—health, recreational, correctional systems, churches, economic development agencies and the like—so that community services can be drawn on when and where required. Unless explicit provision is made for carry-over procedures in all three of these relationships—home, career and community—the barrier which schooling now poses for many of the disadvantaged will remain largely unbreached.

No single set of procedures can be identified as the most effective way to achieve this three-way linkage. The availability of qualified and informed personnel is probably the most crucial element, persons with the time and ability to work closely together at both ends of each of these three relationships and even more closely with those students who can put such outside supportive relationships to good use. Experience does not suggest that the schools should attempt to take over the functions normally performed by the home or community institutions, but rather to provide the major coordinating leadership with respect to students still in school whereby the resources of such institutions can be drawn on more effectively. Unless adequate provision is made for qualified staff at each institutional base, little impact is to be expected.

In terms of the specific job and career needs of disadvantaged young people, the crucial institutional relation is apt to be the tie between the schools and the federal-state Employment Service offices. Other public and private bodies can also be effective in helping such students find job and career openings but chief emphasis needs to be placed on developing close working relations with these offices. In some communities considerable progress has been made in this regard but in many, probably most, little more than perfunctory efforts have been made along this line.

While current thinking among investigators of compensatory school programs has shifted in the direction just described, controversy continues over program specifics. Of the various issues already noted, including development of fundamental academic skills, improved study habits and greater interest in school work, none is more important than the question of how far should direct vocational training be brought into the programs of the secondary schools, a question to which attention turns next. In discussing particular compensatory programs, however, it is important to keep in mind that before any special support measures are withdrawn from students from disadvantaged backgrounds, there must be convincing evidence that they have made necessary progress in the first place. Proposals for putting these students more on their own, holding them to essentially the same standards as nondisadvantaged students, and rewarding or penalizing them on basically the same terms, contain much merit, but only as the conditions surrounding the schooling and postschooling prospects of both groups of students come more closely together. The system of individual incentive, skill acquisition and self development is applicable to the disadvantaged only when the assumptions of the system regarding opportunity to choose, plan, and personally develop are at least remotely approximated. For large numbers of students from disadvantaged backgrounds, this crucial requirement is yet to be met.

The Role of Vocational Education

All the approaches to structural unemployment discussed to this point—policies to reduce mismatching in job markets, wage and related cost barriers, nonwork incentives of income support programs, discriminatory employment practices and basic educational deficiencies—tend to be both long term and roundabout in character. Each has a general though ill-defined contribution to make with respect to this problem and the need for more immediate and direct measures is clear. Among the latter, vocational education has long played a prominent, if rather disappointing, role.

The critical questions with respect to the structural unemployment problem insofar as vocational education is concerned are: first, what contribution can this branch of the country's educational system be expected to make to resolving this problem, and second, should federal funding for vocational education be greatly increased? Historically, training for specific skills in this country has largely been left to private employer initiative. For workers already employed, skills are still mostly acquired informally on the job. Many larger firms, however, have established formal training programs, especially with respect to jobs unique to a given company. Similarly, apprentice programs have provided training in various skilled occupations, notably in the building trades. Private employer sponsorship and financial support have also been crucially important to the numerous private vocational schools and institutes which have been established to provide formal training in a number of special fields such as electronics, printing, textiles and the various clerical skills.

Government supported skill training programs have, until recently, been extremely limited and such efforts as have been made have been chiefly undertaken by state and local governments. Thus the rise in vocational training associated with the recent rapid expansion of community and junior colleges is based only in very small part on federal funding. The first significant support from the federal government came in World War I, but until 1963 federal action was largely limited to occupations in agriculture, home economics, and a few other lines of work. Even in the mid-seventies more than 80 percent of total public expenditures for vocational education came from state and local governments.[13] The 1963 legislation broadened the range of occupations for which federal training funds could be used and appropriations increased fivefold over the next three years, but no widening in the range of occupations was stipulated, expenditures specifically directed to the disadvantaged were miniscule, and the focus of vocational education, except for the addition of office occupations, was still largely limited to the same few fields as before.

In an effort to put vocational education on a broader basis, Congress passed the Vocational Education Amendments of 1968. Provision was made for earmarking of grants-in-aid funds designated by the Congress, specific expenditures for training the disadvantaged were allotted, support for cooperative work-study programs was mandated and the definition of vocational education was widened to

---

13. The total bill for all education in 1973-74 was $96 billion of which public education accounted for $79 billion; in 1972, $2.7 billion was spent on publicly supported vocational education of which state and local governments accounted for 82.5 percent (Levitan, Mangum, and Marshall, *Human Resources and Labor Markets,* p. 233).

include newly emerging, as well as already existing, occupations. Again, much of the thrust of the new legislation has been lost, this time because of the limited support provided in the 1969 Johnson budget and the subsequent Nixon budgets. True, the fiscal year 1971 and 1972 budgets appropriated nearly $500 million for vocational education, nearly double that of 1968, but this was considerably below the $870 million authorized for 1971. After 1975, federal expenditures on vocational education rose markedly and in the 1976-1978 period reached the $725 to $750 million range; even so, the federal share in total public spending on vocational programs remained well below the 29 percent level reached in 1966.[14]

Assessments of Effects

Assessments of the effects of public-supported vocational educational programs, whether viewed in terms of the needs of broad sections of the population or, more narrowly, in terms of the needs of seriously disadvantaged groups, have yielded mixed to mildly positive results. In a careful review of the best available studies comparing college preparatory, vocational, and general curriculum graduates of secondary schools, Michael E. Carbine concluded:

> The conflicting findings are nonetheless sufficient to indicate that, based on the national studies, vocational education apparently yields positive returns to students. . . . Thus, we would judge that vocational education has a small effect on earnings vis-a-vis the secondary academic and general curricula. With one ex-

---

14. *Special Analyses, Budget of the United States Government, Fiscal Year 1978* (Washington: Government Printing Office, 1977), p. 172 and U.S. Office of Education, Department of Health, Education and Welfare, *Annual Reports of the Commissioner of Education* (Washington: Government Printing Office, 1978 and 1979). For a general review of the shifts in vocational education, see Levitan, Mangum, and Marshall, *Human Resources and Labor Markets,* pp. 230-243.

ception, money benefits among the studies range from over $200 to over $800 per year, with most estimates centering around $400 to $600.[15]

The same studies show somewhat higher rates of employment, on average, among young men whose high school background was in the vocational curriculum as compared with those in the academic or general curriculum. One study of three cities, for example, showed that high school graduates from the vocational curriculum experienced 5 to 10 percentage points more time employed during a six-year follow-up period than did the graduates of the academic programs who did not attend college.[16]

As to the effects of vocational education programs on unemployment rates and earnings of disadvantaged, hard-to-employ groups, the findings are less favorable or at least more ambiguous. Historically, these programs were largely built around farming and homemaking skills. The proportion of total enrollments in these two fields has declined markedly as emerging occupations in fields like health, distribution, and "trades and industries" have received more attention. Since the early 1960s, however, the proportion of total enrollments in these latter occupational lines, with the notable exception of office occupations, has not increased appreciably. Of more significance, considerable effort has been expended in recent years to provide vocational education opportunities to disadvantaged groups. While accurate data are unavailable, it appears that these groups accounted

15. Michael E. Carbine, "Evaluations of Vocational Education," Ch. 6 in Leonard A. Lecht, ed., *Evaluating Vocational Education: Policies and Plans for the 1970s* (New York: Praeger, 1974), pp. 79-80.

16. Lecht, ed., *Evaluating Vocational Education,* p. 7, citing Teh-wei Hu, et al., *A Cost Effective Study of Vocational Education: A Comparison of Vocational and Nonvocational Education in Secondary Schools* (University Park, PA: Pennsylvania State University, 1969).

for only a little over 2 percent of all enrollments in 1967 as against about 10 percent in 1974.[17] This shift in focus largely resulted from the legislative requirement that states set aside a minimum of 15 percent of their federal allotment for vocational education for the disadvantaged. In 1975, total Federal Basic Grants to state and local governments came to $428 million of which nearly 18 percent was spent on programs for the disadvantaged; in addition $20 million was made available by the federal government on a nonmatching basis "to support programs and services for persons unable to succeed in regular vocational programs because of poor academic background, lack of motivation, or depressing environmental factors."[18]

Do vocational educational programs significantly improve the subsequent job market experience of disadvantaged workers and, if so, is the improvement worth the higher cost which, exclusive of home economics training, is about double the average costs of general education? Judging from the few careful studies that have been made, the answer to both questions is somewhat more negative than positive and, in contrast to assessments of general compensatory educational programs discussed earlier, recent investigations have marked no shift from this view. True, the latter studies indicate that vocational graduates initially do better in terms of employment and earnings than nonvocational graduates, but over a five- or six-year period the advantage largely disappears and in any event this finding does not bear directly on the experience of disadvantaged vs. nondisadvantaged

17. Office of Education, Department of Health, Education and Welfare, *Annual Report of the Commissioner of Education, Fiscal Year 1975.* The proportion of blacks to total enrollments in vocational education programs comes to about 20 percent, whereas the percentage of blacks to the total population is about 12 percent.

18. *Annual Report of the Commissioner of Education, Fiscal Year 1975,* p. 112. As indicated earlier, the definition of disadvantaged is unclear as is the identity of those who benefit from these special-aid programs.

students.[19] A group of investigators attempted to deal with this latter issue by allowing for differences in socioeconomic status, IQ scores and other personal factors of vocational and comprehensive education programs; their findings showed clear short term, and even some long term, benefits for vocational graduates but any long term gains have been questioned.[20] Merely giving greater weight to vocational education of disadvantaged students without strengthening this aspect of secondary school programs would serve little purpose. Thus, if the discussion were to end here the case for a major expansion in federal government efforts to strengthen vocational education as an approach to structural unemployment would not seem compelling. However, there are several considerations which give this proposal greater strength.

First, the positive effects of these programs on the job status of hard-to-employ groups show up most clearly in periods of prosperity when job vacancies are on the rise. Thus, the National Longitudinal Surveys (the Parnes study) dealing with young men in the 14-26 age group found no significant differences in the earnings of those graduating from different high school curricula in late 1966 when the unemployment rate was rising but significant differences in favor of vocational program graduates in late 1968 when the unemployment rate was falling and labor markets were tightening.[21] This accords with the common sense view that in periods of expanding business, vocational training

19. Michael K. Taussig, "An Economic Analysis of Vocational Education in the New York City High Schools," *Journal of Human Resources,* 3 (Summer 1968), pp. 59-87; Teh-wei Hu, Man Lin Lee, and Ernst W. Stromsdorfer, "Economic Returns to Vocational and Comprehensive High School Graduates," *Journal of Human Resources,* 6 (Winter 1971), pp. 25-47.

20. Haveman, ed., *Decade of Antipoverty Programs,* pp. 173-175.

21. After controlling for a number of social and demographic factors, the study shows that vocational program graduates earned about $400 more a year than the academic program graduates who were in the labor force at the time of the survey. Lecht, *Evaluating Vocational Education,* p. 7.

becomes increasingly important as a means of opening up job opportunities for young people who would otherwise lack saleable labor market skills.

Second, vocational programs have long established ties with the nation's secondary school system and, in the form of institutes, junior colleges and the like, constitute a major element in the country's postsecondary educational system as well. The "establishment" character of these programs makes it difficult for vocational training to adapt to changing needs; witness the continued emphasis on home economics as but one example. Nonetheless, important changes are occurring. While admittedly systematic evidence is lacking that exposure to these programs encourages students to remain in high school or go on to college, nonetheless vocational education often does provide a foundation for further schooling, with over one-half of vocational high school graduates obtaining some additional education after leaving school.[22]

The crucial assumption is that as vocational programs are extended to include a wider range of emerging occupations in the computer, health and service fields, and the relative oversupply of graduates with four-year college degrees becomes more apparent, the skill-training aspect of secondary and postsecondary education will become more generally accepted. This will doubtless induce more "advantaged" students to participate in these programs, too, thereby lessening the benefits in competitive terms accruing to students from disadvantaged backgrounds. Participation could be expected to be on a more equitable basis, however, than in general academic programs, especially if appropriate government safeguards are established.

Third, vocational training is the most effective bridge between school and work available to many students. It is the

22. Lecht, ed., *Evaluating Vocational Education,* p. 9.

one aspect of the secondary school system which most directly concerns employers, as evidenced by the fact that a
number of programs are based on close collaboration between employers and the schools. If carefully designed, these
programs can provide entree to job opportunities for a wide
variety of students, including those lacking in verbal or
quantitative skills. Even though previous efforts to help
students of the latter sort in this regard have been quite
limited, some positive results have been achieved. More
vigorous efforts, if carefully developed and implemented,
would seem eminently justified.

There are certain aspects of vocational training with
respect to reducing the amount of structural unemployment
which are more promising than others. One is to give more
weight to work-study arrangements which are carried out
with the cooperation of individual firms or employer groups.
Until recently, enrollments in these programs have hardly exceeded 300,000, but a goal of over a million would not seem
excessive as broader acceptance by employers is achieved. In
this connection the Carnegie Council Report referred to
earlier recommended that:

> Classroom vocational education at the high school
> level should be deemphasized in favor of training con-
> ducted under employer auspices, apprenticeship, work-
> experience programs, cooperative [work-study] educa-
> tion, and other programs to take the student into the
> community.[23]

Following the lead of earlier work by Willard Wirtz and the
National Manpower Institute, the Carnegie group also supported the establishment in major cities of community
education-work councils through which school officials,

---

23. Carnegie Council on Policy Studies in Higher Education, p. 141. The title of the
chapter dealing with this subject is Vocational Education: Change Everything, Including
the Name.

employers, members of labor unions and members of the public engage collaboratively in developing and administering education-work programs.[24]

Another proposal is to broaden the range of occupational lines for which training is available still further, particularly areas in which job opportunities are expected to multiply over the next 10 to 20 years. Some progress, as already noted, has been made in this direction, but much yet remains to be done. Similarly, there is need for more systematic screening, advising, and follow up of participants from the point of initial entry in a training program to placement in a job with at least some career potential. The lack of adequate guidance and progress assessment is especially costly in the case of students coming from disadvantaged backgrounds. These considerations chiefly apply to students in secondary schools and postsecondary schools offering other than general academic work but, with some qualifications, they apply to adults in vocational education programs as well.

Principal responsibility for moving vocational schools and programs in these directions lies with the federal government since it commands both the breadth of viewpoint and the source of funds needed to mount an effective strategy. Beyond the general lines noted above, there is little agreement on specific next steps, so an experimental approach backed up by careful research and continuing appraisal seems the only prudent course to follow. This is not to say that vigorous federal efforts to strengthen and broaden vocational education are not called for; to the contrary, a pronounced increase in such efforts would mark an important step in dealing with structural unemployment and related problems.

---

24. Ibid., p. 125.

Chapter 8
Public Service Employment Programs

Government efforts to deal with unemployment by direct but selective job creation has a long history, but this aspect of public policy was largely forgotten as Keynesian ideas concerning aggregate demand management became more widely accepted. Thus, in the early 1960s, attention centered on expanding demand by such means as the 1962 investment tax credit and the 1964 personal and corporate income tax cuts. Subsequently, with preparation for the Vietnam War inducing a sharp rise in aggregate demand, a few selective measures were introduced which were aimed at providing not only training but some limited forms of work experience and public service employment. In 1967 the government launched the Concentrated Employment Program (CEP) which sought to provide "one-stop" training and other services to disadvantaged workers in inner-city areas who were subject to the worst employment and income conditions and, additionally, to induce private employers to hire such workers from these severely depressed areas.

In 1968 a still more ambitious effort, the Jobs Opportunities in the Business Sector (JOBS), was undertaken to induce private industry to hire disadvantaged workers. Under this program, which was administered by a group of national business leaders, the government covered any training or other special costs entailed in employing nonexperienced,

137

nonskilled workers. Most of the employers participating in this program were large corporations and approximately two-thirds of the cooperating firms did so without any compensation from the government. By the end of the 1960s there were nearly twenty federal programs, each constituting an individual category administered from Washington but all aimed primarily at the training and employment problems of the disadvantaged.[1]

Public Service Employment Programs in the 1970s

After 1969 and the advent of the Nixon administration, the federal government moved to shift major responsibility for allocating funds among these diverse programs to state and local government units and to "decategorize" most of the programs. The basic legislation of this period was the Comprehensive Employment and Training Act (CETA) passed in December 1973. Under Titles I and II of this Act, state and local governments were given federal financial assistance to undertake a wide range of manpower services including public service jobs for unemployed or underemployed workers in areas of substantial unemployment. Job creation was given little weight, however, until unemployment began to increase with the onset of the 1973-1975 recession. In 1974, with the unemployment rate above 8 percent, Congress added Title VI to CETA which authorized a broad one-year countercyclical Public Service Employment (PSE) program. Unemployment fell only slightly in the subsequent recovery and, in passing the Emergency Jobs Program Extension Act of 1976 (EJPEA), Congress continued the Title VI public service job provision

---

1. William Mirengoff and Lester Rindler, *The Comprehensive Employment and Training Act: Impact on People, Places, Programs: An Interim Report* (Washington: National Academy of Sciences, 1976), p. iii.

along with Title II which was aimed more directly at structural unemployment.

In designing the 1976 Act, Congress sought to resolve a number of difficulties experienced under CETA. First and most important, it was concluded that many of the workers who were eligible for aid under Title VI and even under Title II were from nondisadvantaged backgrounds. Second, there was considerable evidence that local governments were simply substituting CETA workers for regular employees to the point where there was little or no overall net job creation. Third, it was felt that many of the jobs secured under both titles were of too long duration and provided little or no chance of leading to regular employment in either the private or public sector. Finally, it was concluded that under CETA local sponsors enjoyed too wide a latitude with respect not only to public service employment but to other aspects of manpower training and development as well. Both on grounds of more efficient organization and clearer direction of policy it was decided that a move back towards greater federal control was indicated.

The Emergency Jobs Program Extension Act of 1976 was primarily aimed at the first of these four concerns. EJPEA required that prime sponsors limit hirings to AFDC recipients, unemployment insurance beneficiaries and exhaustees, and other low-income persons unemployed 15 weeks or longer. This tightening of eligibility requirements reduced the pool of potential applicants for most new PSE positions from about 20 million to 4.5 million persons; as a result, the proportion of those hired for projects from disadvantaged backgrounds increased significantly. However, the tighter eligibility requirements applied not to Title II positions, but only to newly created positions under Title VI and to half of the regular, so-called sustainment jobs under this title; sustainment jobs accounted for about 40 percent of all Title VI project positions. Moreover, in actual practice, many ineligibles were hired under the public service employment programs. Emphasis was placed on speedy expansion of programs and local sponsors were permitted to undertake projects that simply extended activities already in existence. As a result, little progress was made in reducing the substitution of federal for local outlays and in increasing net job creation. Nor were effective steps taken to shorten the duration of jobs under EJPEA, establish projects entailing transferable skills, or develop a more clear-cut set of policy priorities.

The Reauthorization Act of 1978 which extended CETA for four years was in large part addressed to these issues, but the changes were relatively minor. The tighter eligibility requirements that had been limited to Title VI were extended to what was now designated as Title II-D, the permanent program combining public service employment with training for the structurally unemployed. The 1978 Reauthorization Act also lowered the average wage that could be paid participants, presumably on the assumption this would lessen the substitution danger. Greater authority, in addition, was given the Department of Labor to enforce eligibility rules and prevent substitution. Under the new law, for example, prime sponsors were made clearly accountable for any misspent funds. Finally, the reauthorization act required sponsors to assess the employability of each participant and provide employment counseling, training, or other services wherever necessary; while the funds provided for this purpose are meager (5 percent of allotted funds received for training under Title VI after fiscal 1979), this could prove to be the single most important provision of the 1978 law. The changing relationships between the government's public service employment and its various training programs during the 1970s are shown in figure 8-1.

Figure 8-1
Outlays for Training and Employment Activities

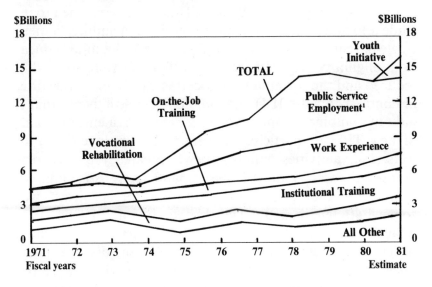

Service Years for Training and Employment Activities

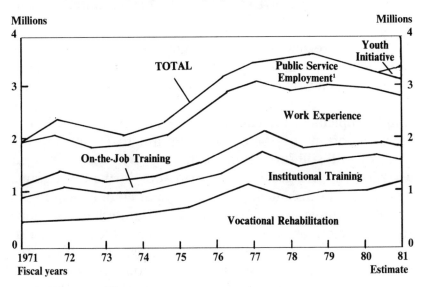

Source: The Budget of the U.S. Government, Fiscal Year 1981, p. 231.
1. Total Public Service Employment Activities

In a number of respects, however, the 1978 statute loosen-ed rather than tightened eligibility requirements and project terms. Targeting rules under Title II-D were broadened to in-clude a long list of disadvantaged workers including women, single parents, older workers and persons with limited educa-tion; eligibility requirements under Title VI were somewhat reduced and the formula for allocating funds under this title, in contrast to Title II-D, was made less restrictive in that it did not combine income level with unemployment; only half of new Title VI participants were to be employed on pro-jects, i.e., activities entailing newly created jobs, whereas before all new Title VI participants were so required. Moreover, the permissible duration of projects was somewhat lengthened. The broad intent of the 1978 Reauthorization Act was to limit public service employment programs almost entirely to the long term, disadvantaged unemployed, but the specific provisions of the statute put this outcome in considerable doubt. The foregoing aspects of the 1973, 1976 and 1978 CETA legislation are summarized in table 8-1.

This brief review of recent developments in public service employment programs points to a number of specific changes which would strengthen federal policies in this area. For the most part these consist of proposals which would simply implement the changes in CETA just reviewed. The most important of these proposals are to (1) narrow the focus of PSE still further on the most severely disadvantaged workers, (2) give greater weight to jobs in these programs which would subsequently lead to regular employment in the private or public sector, (3) shorten the duration of such jobs for the same reason, (4) put more emphasis on training in skills and related work abilities as an aspect of PSE pro-grams, (5) focus these programs more completely on newly created jobs so as to minimize the substitution of federal for state and local funds, and (6) establish more effective

Table 8-1
Persons Eligible for Public Service Employment Programs and Participants Under the 1973, 1976 and 1978 CETA Legislation

	Eligibility requirements	Potentially eligible population (millions)	Participants Date	Participants Number
Under 1973 CETA Legislation				
Title II	Unemployed 30 days or more; or underemployed	20.2	June 1976	74,000
Title VI	Same as Title II, above	20.2	June 1976	171,000
Under 1976 EJPEA				
Title II	Same as Title II, above	20.2	March 1978	129,000
Title VI: Projects	Unemployed 15 weeks or more and member of low-income family; AFDC recipients	4.4	March 1978	347,000
Title VI: Sustainment Half of new enrollees for regular Title VI positions	Same as Title VI projects	4.4	March 1978	82,000
Half of new enrollees for regular Title VI positions and participants carried over from before October 1976	Same as Title II, above	20.2	March 1978	184,000

Table 8-1 (continued)

	Eligibility requirements	Potentially eligible population (millions)	Date	Participants Number
Under 1978 CETA Amendments				
II-D	Unemployed 15 weeks and member of family with income of less than 70 percent of BLS family budget; or member of family receiving AFDC or SSI	4.0	March 1979	222,600
VI	Unemployed 10 of last 12 weeks and unemployed at time of determination; and an AFDC or SSI recipient or member of family with income of less than 100 percent of BLS lower level family budget	6.0	March 1979	316,900

Source: William Mirengoff et. al., *CETA: Assessment of Public Service Employment Programs* (Washington: National Academy of Sciences, 1980), pp. 16 and 20-21; data for 1978 CETA Amendments supplied by Office of Employment and Training, U.S. Department of Labor.

monitoring and enforcement controls to insure projected program results. On first consideration, changes along these six lines appear quite straightforward and virtually unassailable; on further examination, however, they pose a number of important, still-to-be-answered questions which warrant careful attention. These questions appear in quite a different light depending on whether they are viewed in a narrow or broad perspective.

Relationship to Other Types of Unemployment

One major unresolved issue is how PSE programs for dealing with structural unemployment can best be fitted into broader federal efforts to deal with other types of unemployment. In the various legislative phases for CETA, for example, no distinction was initially drawn between structural and cyclical unemployment regarding PSE programs; next the attempt was made to draw a sharp line between the former and the latter (Titles II and VI respectively); finally PSE was limited to structural unemployment alone, or more specifically to the severely disadvantaged unemployed or underemployed as a separate and distinguishable group.

The difficulty with this last formulation is that the extent and nature of structural unemployment varies with changes in the general level of economic activity and limiting PSE programs to a given group is likely to prove most difficult. It is safe to say that if unemployment rises much above 6 percent, steps will be taken to provide public employment on a broadened basis in any case; the issue, then, is how such an expanded program can best be related to already ongoing PSE programs.[2]

---

2. In this discussion, public service employment refers only to government employment programs aimed at providing jobs targeted on disadvantaged workers who face unusually serious structural barriers to employment; public employment refers to other government programs aimed at counteracting cyclical or longer term swings in employment on a non-targeted basis.

The most promising approach is to distinguish between the kind of unemployment which requires relatively intensive support efforts and the kind that does not. As a practical matter, the greater part of unemployment resulting from marked cyclical declines or sustained downward trends in business activity cannot be dealt with on anything approaching an individual case basis; nor would this type of unemployment in any event call for such selective treatment. Adhering to a distinction of this sort would admittedly be no easy task; determining who would qualify for the targeted special support type of employment could not escape controversy. On both practical and conceptual grounds, however, the distinction would seem altogether appropriate.

The same issue arises in even more extreme form regarding the long term increase in youth unemployment. In fiscal year 1977, for example, federal aid providing jobs for young people came to about $2.5 billion in fiscal 1977; in fiscal 1979 the total (which included some training as well) came to over $4.5 billion and even in the face of subsequent budget cutting efforts this total is expected to increase sharply over the next few years.[3] The sheer scale of this effort would make it necessary to limit the more intensive, specially designed type of government employment program to the neediest young people confronting the most serious barriers to employment.

The important distinction underlying this approach to Public Service Employment programs is not between structural and nonstructural unemployment but within the structural category itself. Many persons, particularly younger workers, can properly be included among the structurally unemployed but certainly could not be classified among the most severely disadvantaged, no matter how broadly the term is defined. How far the government should attempt to

---

3. *The Budget of the United States Government, Fiscal Year 1981* (Washington: Government Printing Office, 1980), p. 235.

go in providing public created jobs for such less disadvantaged workers and on what terms is a separate issue, depending on what overall strategies are chosen for dealing with cyclical declines or other sources of unemployment. The essential point is that, to be effective, the type of public service employment needed by the most seriously disadvantaged among the structurally unemployed or underemployed should be sharply differentiated from government-created job opportunities for less needy workers.

Defining the Goal and Devising a Strategy

Once it is agreed that Public Service Employment programs, as opposed to other more general government job creation efforts, should be limited to the most needy disadvantaged workers, the requirements for effective public action in this area begin to fall into place. Like most other measures designed to help those most in need, the aim of any PSE program of this sort can be defined as providing the most severely disadvantaged with practical, attainable opportunities to find and keep permanent, regular jobs. While differing in important respects from one individual and situation to the next, the most promising strategy for achieving this goal is to identify the steps which a person needs to take to qualify for regular work and to make sure that the steps are in fact made available. Persons would of course come in at different levels, but since the program would be limited to the severely disadvantaged, many would have to start at a relatively general and fundamental level. Subsequently, more advanced, specialized work experience and training would be made available. Chief weight, however, would need to be placed on giving every individual participating in the program a genuine, clear-cut opportunity to move towards regular employment with definite incentives provided at each step in the process. Without the latter, the essential element of motivation would almost surely be lacking.

The most ambitious effort that has been undertaken along these lines is the five-year program known as the National Supported Work Demonstration project which was launched in 1975 at a cost of $82 million by the federal government and the Ford Foundation. The project was aimed at helping four groups facing long-standing employment problems find stable jobs in regular work: long term recipients of AFDC, ex-addicts who had been in drug treatment, ex-offenders who had been released from custody, and young school dropouts, some of whom had also been delinquents. The focus of the program was the assigning of participants to temporary unskilled but specially structured jobs in such areas as housing rehabilitation, building maintenance and clerical work. Participants were placed in crews of their peers and were supervised by staff members who were familiar with their backgrounds and work histories. Performance standards were gradually increased through the participation period until they matched conditions in the regular labor market. Prompt and steady attendance as well as good performance was rewarded by a system of bonuses.

A carefully designed cost-benefit analysis of the program's effects in 10 of the 15 demonstration sites was carried out by means of frequent interviews with 6,616 participants over varying periods up to 3 years. The results of this analysis were mixed. On the one hand, the program was found to be successful in enabling a significant number of welfare mothers find permanent employment after their subsidized work periods were completed; in their cases, from the perspective of society as a whole, long term benefits exceeded costs by over $8,000 per AFDC participant. The members of the ex-addict group, while making less striking gains, also received long term benefits relative to costs, particularly with respect to lowered participation in property and drug crimes. With respect to the two other groups, however, the young school dropouts and the ex-offenders, no major progress in increasing employment was achieved.[4]

The main policy implication of this project is that for certain groups facing long-standing employment problems, a carefully structured work experience resembling usual job conditions and work standards as closely as possible can mean the difference between unstable, low-level jobs and persistent unemployment on the one hand, and on the other, permanent jobs in the regular labor market. There is now substantial evidence that many disadvantaged workers have the necessary motivation and general qualities to meet normal job requirements if they are given the means to do so. For others, these same procedures do not suffice, but even in their case further efforts in this direction deserve serious consideration.

The Demand Component

While the abilities and interests of participants are the major determinants of an approach to public service employment programs along these lines, the requirements and opportunities obtaining in the regular job market are hardly less important. Except as a stopgap measure, and an extremely expensive one at that, little would be gained from a PSE program for the severely disadvantaged if work opportunities adapted to the abilities and interests of participants were not subsequently available. Precise projections of regular job openings that would be available in a given locality or region for a year or two ahead would of course not be possible, but a rough matching of the future re-

4. *New York Times,* February 28, 1980. For details, see Peter Kemper et al., Manpower Demonstration Research Corporation, *Summary of Findings of the National Supported Work Demonstration* (Cambridge, MA: Ballinger Publishing Co., 1980).

quirements of employers and the number of expected completers of PSE programs would be feasible.

If any serious effort were made of this nature, something which for the most part has yet to be done, the implications for the design and implementation of these programs would be far reaching. In periods of strong business expansion, a shift in emphasis to meeting the job requirements of employers in the private and public sector as job opportunities became more abundant would be especially important. Even in these circumstances, it is by no means certain that specialized skilled training immediately demanded by particular employers would be the proper focus for a given PSE program if for no other reason than that the backgrounds, abilities and interests of program participants would vary so widely. Nonetheless, if finding regular work remains the crucial test, the dependence of PSE on acceptance by employers and therefore on their needs is evident. Viewed in this light, a program of subsidized employment which culminated in a apprentice training opportunity would seem highly desirable. In this sense at least the job preparation needs of severely disadvantaged workers are no different from other long term but less disadvantaged unemployed or underemployed persons.

Still another implication is that if the number of subsidized PSE job holders were limited by the number and composition of regular job openings, public service employment would presumably be sharply restricted in most localities. Not only would this call for a further tightening in eligibility requirements in determining who should be included in the severely disadvantaged unemployed and underemployed pool of workers, but local authorities would also need to be able to set still tighter requirements if sufficient regular market job opportunities are not expected. In periods of strong business expansion this will be less of a problem than if unemployment is generally rising or has become widespread. In the latter environment more sweeping types of public employment programs would doubtless prove necessary; programs appropriate to such an economic environment, however, should be sharply distinguished from the kind of PSE program outlined here.

The Substitution Issue

Despite continuing efforts to minimize the substitution of federal for local dollars in public service employment programs, the danger of this occurring still exists. Earlier studies indicated that the substitution effect was quite high. In the 1976 investigation by Alan Fechter, for example, this effect was said to be in the range of 50 percent; in the 1978 study by the National Research Council, on the other hand, it was estimated to average about 35 percent and in the 1979 survey volume, *Evaluating Manpower Training Programs,* George Johnson's estimate came to less than 20 percent.[5] While it is evident that the initial estimates were too high, the substitution question remains a serious one.

Both the Emergency Jobs Programs Act of 1976 and the CETA Reauthorization Act of 1978 were aimed at reducing the substitution effects of public service employment programs. Under this legislation, most new hires were to be employed in short-duration projects outside existing government services, prime sponsors were encouraged to make contracts with private nonprofit organizations and government agencies on the understanding they would undertake new activities, the permissible average wage was set low enough

---

5. Alan Fechter, *Public Employment Programs* (Washington: The Urban Institute, 1976); National Research Council, *CETA: Manpower Programs Under Local Control* (Washington: National Academy of Sciences, 1978), p. 179; Farrell E. Bloch, ed., *Evaluating Manpower Training Programs* (Greenwich, CN: JAI Press, 1979), essay by George E. Johnson, "The Labor Market Displacement Effect in the Analysis of the Net Impact of Manpower Training Programs," pp. 227-254. It should be emphasized that the Johnson essay is confined to the effects of manpower training programs alone.

($7,200 in annual terms in 1979) to induce greater participation by nonprofit organizations and, finally, the Department of Labor was authorized to establish new controls and enforcement procedures to prevent substitution by local prime sponsors.

As noted earlier, the CETA legislation now on the books undercuts these provisions in a number of ways, most notably by providing that only half of Title VI funds be used for projects as opposed to maintaining already existing activities and, what is more serious, the term "project" is defined in such a way so as to include almost any kind of activity.[6] Still further tightening along lines already taken are needed if the substitution danger is to be dealt with effectively.

There remains the question whether changes of this sort, being limited to detailed features of the law and its administration, would in fact significantly reduce the substitution effects of PSE programs. The chances are high they would not. Even with these changes, the sheer size and scope of these programs would almost certainly result in sponsors stretching the rules and substituting federal for local funds. The wider the range of skills and backgrounds of PSE participants, the greater would be the inducement to use the federal monies in this way. This is but another example of the difficulties that will persist as long as PSE programs are aimed at groups other than those facing the most serious economic and social barriers to employment.

The other basic requirement for minimizing the substitution danger is to confine PSE to the kinds of work and training experience for which demand prospects are most promising and regular job openings most likely to exist. While the existing legislation embraces this general objective, provision

6. National Research Council, *CETA: Manpower Programs Under Local Control,* p. 26.

for effective implementation is lacking. Indeed, the 1978 Reauthorization Act marks a step backward in this regard in that subsequent to fiscal 1979, only 5 percent of funds are allotted to training as against the 10 percent limit that existed before. Unless PSE programs can help participants develop the specific and basic abilities required in job areas where vacancies are likely to occur, the problem of substitution can be expected to persist.

Individual Motivation and Career Entry

Much controversy remains over the question whether PSE enrollees generally lack the motivation necessary to find regular jobs. Such evidence as exists does not provide a convincing answer to this question, the results being too mixed to yield a firm conclusion. It is possible, however, to identify some of the circumstances where individual motivation is likeliest to be positive. Perhaps most important, there has to be assurance that the PSE experience can be expected to yield worthwhile benefits in a reasonably short period of time if the individual meets performance standards satisfactorily. It is wholly understandable why many participants, given their prior backgrounds and experiences, would require more than promises of long term and necessarily vague benefits. Not even the likelihood of finding regular and satisfying work in a year or so could always be counted on to provide the necessary motivation to do well in a given PSE program. Indeed, it seems quite incontrovertible that, lacking this prospect, the necessary motivation will probably not be forthcoming. Unless the programs contain this element and do so in ways that are convincing to the average enrollee, expenditures on the programs will be largely wasted.

The other side of the coin is that if participants cannot meet the performance standards of the programs successfully, employers can hardly be expected to take them on as actual or even potential regular employees. Just as these workers need confidence that regular jobs are in prospect, employers need confidence that in a reasonably short time new hires can meet minimum standards of performance.

These considerations underscore the importance of a major theme of this study: workers facing serious barriers to employment cannot be dealt with effectively in large homogeneous groups; fully individualized treatment in all cases is of course out of the question, but since account has to be taken of differing needs and plans, reasonably close track must be maintained of the progress of each worker. Lacking this, neither current participants nor potential employers are likely to have sufficient confidence in the programs to keep them on a solid basis. Admittedly, not even this approach will assure favorable results, but at least it will heighten the chances for success.

The specific features of a possible approach to PSE along these lines were outlined earlier in this chapter. The key consideration was to provide participants with a series of clearly defined steps whereby they could qualify for regular, unsubsidized work in either the private or public sector. In this way, emphasis would be placed on enlisting individual worker effort to achieve regular job status—public policy would provide the opportunity in successive phases but the initiative at each level would be left to the individual. Any attempt to put a program along these lines on a mass basis could hardly escape failure.

The principal element in an approach built along such highly restrictive lines is the kind of training which should be provided. Thus, the government's public service employment programs have to be viewed in the context of its broader responsibilities in the training area, the subject to which attention now turns.

Chapter 9
Government Training Programs

The emergence of government training programs in the 1960s as the principal means for reducing structural unemployment squared with both popular views and logical analysis. In an environment of high employment, what better way to help the hard-to-employ than to equip them with essential skills and sufficient work experience to enable them to find worthwhile jobs?

The first major legislation of this period, the Manpower Development and Training Act (MDTA) passed in 1962, was primarily designed to retool workers who already had job experience but whose skills had become obsolete. This focus quickly shifted, however, when business conditions improved and it became apparent that the unemployment problem was largely confined to persons who lacked any marketable skills or any sustained work experience, notably teenagers, minority workers, and the "permanently" unemployed or grossly underemployed. An early instance of this change in emphasis came in 1963 when MDTA was amended to permit the youth training category to increase from 5 percent to 25 percent of total enrollments. With some temporary shifts and even reversals in policy, the government moved still further in this direction in the remainder of the 1960s and during the 1970s.

Other trends in the development of government training programs during these two decades were less clear-cut. As long as business conditions remained buoyant, as during much of the 1960s, emphasis centered almost exclusively on training in specific skills as the means for opening up jobs to the hard-to-employ. Even during this period, however, it became evident that many workers faced major barriers in the search for regular employment. As a consequence, efforts were made to couple training with related services such as counseling, job placement and temporary work experience. By the mid-1970s, as indicated in the preceding chapter, more emphasis had come to be placed on providing temporary jobs than on providing training, first as a way of dealing with structural unemployment and then with cyclical unemployment. At the end of the 1970s somewhat greater attention was once again being given to training in specific skills, but this was primarily viewed as an element in subsidized work programs, with the chief emphasis still placed on providing the disadvantaged among the unemployed with temporary job opportunities.

The decline in support of training programs was largely due to mounting skepticism about their effectiveness. While the necessary data for definitive evaluations were not available, most of the studies completed by the early 1970s yielded quite unfavorable conclusions, with estimates of benefit-cost ratios running close to zero. Ironically, as the focus of public policy shifted from training to jobs, more adequate data became available and later studies revealed that the training programs of the 1960s resulted in a modest but significant net increase in participants' earnings.[1] By the end of the 1970s, interest in training as an approach to the problem of hardcore unemployment somewhat revived.

---

1. Farrell E. Bloch, ed., *Evaluating Manpower Training Programs,* essay by George E. Johnson, pp. 227-254, citing studies for the U.S. Department of Labor by Orley Ashenfelter (1973) and Thomas F. Cooley and Edward C. Prescott (1972).

Looking to the 1980s, the principal questions confronting public policymakers will be much the same regarding government training programs as those considered earlier regarding public service employment: What are the effects on these programs of changes in the overall level of business activity? To what extent should such programs be targeted to the most severely disadvantaged workers? Have the programs resulted in the displacement of other workers to a significant degree and if so, how can such displacement effects be minimized? How can government training programs most effectively promote entry of participants into regular work in the private and public sector? Finally, how can the programs most effectively contribute to improved motivation on the part of participants?

Policy responses to these questions can be expected to be hardly less tentative and controversial than in the case of public service employment programs, since the government's approach to training has shifted frequently over the past twenty years and the amount of scientific evaluation of results has been extremely limited. The few policy recommendations that emerge from this experience and these studies, while differing in certain respects, follow the same general lines in both sets of programs.

The Effects of High Employment

In accordance with generally accepted views, government policy can be expected to shift from a job creation emphasis in periods of low employment to a skill improvement emphasis in periods of high employment. This follows from the fact that expansions in public employment are called for when the general level of unemployment is high but a broadening of manpower training is needed as labor supplies become scarcer. In good measure this was the story of the 1960s and the 1970s; in the earlier decade, the trend in unemployment was downward and emphasis was appropriately placed on training, whereas in the later decade the opposite trend occurred and emphasis was quite rightly shifted to job creation.

As a guide to policy, however, this distinction can easily be carried too far. For one thing, total employment can rise strongly but the unemployment rate remains too high to justify any such marked change in policy direction. Even if the overall jobless rate were to decline significantly, the job picture for many disadvantaged workers may remain very unfavorable and, for these workers, continuation of some special type of public employment program would be essential.

As to expanding government training efforts in periods of strong business expansion, a similar skepticism would be justified. To the exent such efforts were concentrated on the severely disadvantaged, the increased emphasis on training would be altogether appropriate since it is in these periods that special training opportunities for the hard-to-employ would be most likely to succeed. Responsibility for training other workers in these circumstances, on the other hand, could be largely shifted to private employers since, in periods of expanding business, greater reliance can be placed on normal market processes to fulfill the training and job placement needs of most workers. The further point also needs to be kept in mind that government training programs, in large part in contradistinction to public employment programs, are designed to meet longer term requirements of workers and employers; once in place, sharp reversals in their scope and direction would not be desirable.

Training Program Links to Job Vacancies

The more relevant question to consider is whether there are some types of government training activities which are better adapted to periods of high employment than others, that is, to periods when job openings are multiplying and career prospects are generally improving. In such periods, training programs that are focused most explicitly on filling the labor-upgrading needs and longer term career openings of private and public employers are particularly appropriate. Unfortunately, a few of the earlier programs and even fewer of those in effect in the 1976-1979 upswing had this aim. Only two of the programs, Public Service Careers (PSC) and Apprenticeship Outreach Program (AOP), were directly aimed from their inception at getting enrollees into career-related positions. PSC was designed

> . . . to relieve shortages of professional personnel in human service activities [health, education, neighborhood redevelopment, etc.] to meet the need of the unemployed and underemployed for meaningful jobs with career ladder possibilities.[2]

At first this program, then known as New Careers, was limited to human services jobs in the public sector, but in 1970 it was expanded to include a wide range of positions in state and local government agencies. Under this program the federal government undertook, through grants and other means, to place disadvantaged adults and younger workers in permanent jobs in the public sector. The aim was to get them into positions with career potential and to this end federal funds were made available to help defray extra training costs of these workers.

The focus of AOP was on helping disadvantaged workers meet requirements for entrance into apprenticeship programs, chiefly in the construction trades. This has been achieved by allocating federal funds to such groups as

---

2. *Manpower Report of the President, 1968* (Washington: Government Printing Office, 1969), p. 102.

building trades councils, the National Urban League and the Workers' Defense League which have agreed to provide guidance, training and other aids to minority group workers who otherwise would not qualify for or even know about apprentice training opportunities. Such opportunities were already generally available in the less skilled lines of work such as the "trowel trades" in the construction field, but not in lines requiring considerable technical preparation such as the electrical, plumbing and mechanical trades. AOP, accordingly, has given special emphasis to helping workers from disadvantaged backgrounds gain access to these hard-to-enter careers.

Several other programs have sought to provide direct entry to jobs, chiefly in private industry, but they have placed little weight on longer term career elements. The Manpower and Development Act On-the-Job Training program (MDTA-OJT) was something of an exception in the latter regard; under this program, every participant has been given a job in a private company with the assurance of some training and at least the possibility of permanent employment. Other programs have also provided placement in specific companies, but in entry-level jobs only, with a bare modicum of training and no assurance of permanence. Both the Work Incentive Program (WIN, now known as Work Experience) and the Job Opportunities in the Business Sector (JOBS) programs have made explicit provision for giving employment and training opportunities to disadvantaged workers but in neither case has the relationship been effectively implemented.

In the case of WIN, beneficiaries under the Aid to Families with Dependent Children program (AFDC) are required to register for referral either to a job, to a training program, or to some other supportive service. At first the effort to combine work and welfare, which began in the early 1960s, emphasized voluntary job search and participation in training, but the state and local welfare agencies were ill-prepared to handle the undertaking and the incentives provided enrollees to get off welfare and accept employment proved generally ineffective. A more basic difficulty was that job openings for these workers, even in the favorable environment of the 1960s, were limited and the training programs often did not qualify them for such openings. In the 1970s, especially after the Talmadge amendments of 1971, the emphasis shifted from voluntary to required job finding procedures and from training and related supportive services to job placement and immediate job search aids. With this shift in focus, in the words of one survey,

> . . . public policy has virtually abandoned earlier rhetoric about helping welfare recipients to achieve financial independence, opting instead to move beneficiaries into any job as soon as possible.[3]

Viewed in short-run terms, this reorientation of WIN met with some success: by 1978, registrants in the program had risen to over 2 million and nearly 300,000 found jobs as against 1.2 million registrants and 137,000 job finders in the boom year of 1973. As an approach to the problem of structural unemployment, however, the difficulty was and still is that the unemployment-prone groups—blacks, young workers, women and older workers—were less often represented among job entrants than among program registrants by substantial margins. In fiscal 1978, for example, there were 124,000 fewer job entrants among women, and 140,000 fewer among blacks, than registrants whereas job entrants exceeded registrants by substantial margins in the cases of men and whites. Efforts to induce employers to take on women and black registrants, much less the more severely disadvantaged members among these groups, by tax credits, intensive information campaigns, and the like, have

---

3. Levitan, Mangum, and Marshall, *Human Resources and Labor Markets,* p. 337.

had few observable results.[4] Thus an effective approach to combining work and welfare still remains to be found.

Though the initial orientation of JOBS was very different from that of the WIN program, it too failed to establish effective links for participants between employment and other components of job placement. This occurred despite the fact that, from its inception in 1968, one of the guiding principles of JOBS was to integrate work opportunities for the disadvantaged with on-the-job training. Under the slogan "hire now, train later," a much-publicized national effort was launched to induce major employers to take on disadvantaged workers and provide them with the training necessary to qualify for regular employment; firms signing appropriate contracts were to be compensated for the special training costs involved but only about one-third of the participating companies chose this procedure.

While adequate data are lacking, investigations of the program reveal great variability among firms in the range of training and supportive services. In summing up the findings on this aspect of the JOBS program, the Wharton Industrial Research Unit study concluded:

> Overall, the quantity and quality of training and other services appears to have been [relatively] superior in the contract segment of the program, but [even] the record of the contract participants in providing services contracted and compensated for was far from good.[5]

The study notes that prior to 1970 there was some tendency among firms which signed JOBS contracts to provide a wider range of career-oriented job opportunities for disadvantaged

---

4. *Employment and Training Report of the President, 1977,* pp. 58-63, and *Employment and Training Report of the President, 1979,* pp. 53-54.

5. Charles R. Perry, *The Impact of Government Manpower Programs in General and on Minorities and Women* (Philadelphia: Industrial Research Unit, The Wharton School, University of Pennsylvania, 1975), p. 191.

employees who would have been hired in any case but for whom little in the way of prejob training or supportive services would have been provided; even among these employers, however, the benefits on this score were apparently meager.[6]

The factors leading to this generally unfavorable outcome are not altogether clear, but two considerations deserve mention. First, since the JOBS program sought to provide mass employment to large numbers of disadvantaged workers on virtually a crash basis, the effort centered largely on entry-level jobs, despite any career planning pronouncements to the contrary. Second, the downswing in business and the sharp rise in unemployment that occurred after 1969 induced a number of key firms to withdraw from the JOBS program while layoffs at other firms blocked further efforts to provide even entry-level jobs to these workers.

Programs such as MDTA-Institutional and the Concentrated Employment Program (CEP) also developed few effective links with employment opportunities, much less longer term career opportunities for disadvantaged participants; but since they provided specific skills they at least increased the potential for these workers to find regular employment. These programs operated on the assumption that if disadvantaged workers could acquire the qualities demanded by employers, additional job finding aids specially designed for such workers would generally be unnecessary; existing facilities provided by the Employment Service and other agencies were deemed generally sufficient once these workers had achieved job-readiness status.[7] Studies of the post-training experience of MDTA-

---

6. Ibid., p. 195.

7. The Opportunities Industrialization Centers program (OIC) has a similar training emphasis but lack of data makes any generalization about its employment impact extremely hazardous.

Institutional participants indicate that the program has helped enrollees, especially women, who were previously unemployed find work, but has done less for those already employed. Moreover, speaking particularly of disadvantaged participants, it is clear that the program has been largely limited to entry-level jobs.[8]

The CEP program placed heavy emphasis on inducing employers to provide jobs for its participants, but its success in this regard has been very limited. This program was designed as a "one-stop" coordinating agency to help disadvantaged workers in severely depressed localities, chiefly large inner-city areas, find job openings and secure the training and related services to qualify for such openings. Actual responsibility for meeting their training and other job finding needs was left to subcontracting agencies, with CEP serving largely as a coordinating office. This organizational structure militated against achieving quick or easily demonstrable successes. Training was frequently not carried to the point where enrollees could step into any but the very lowest grade jobs and employers became increasingly reluctant to take on workers from the program. After 1969, most of CEP's job placement and related functions were transferred to the federal-state Employment Service and attention shifted to placing workers with more acceptable job qualifications. Today, general responsibility in this regard is vested in the local prime sponsors under the CETA legislation while immediate implementation of whatever remains of the "one-stop" system of referrals is largely performed by the Employment Service offices.

The record shows that only a few of the government's training programs are explicitly designed to promote a career-entry type of job placement, the kind of training

---

8. The Job Corps program, which also has a training focus, is discussed at a later point in this chapter.

orientation that is best suited to a high employment environment. In periods of strong business expansion a shift in emphasis in this direction seems clearly warranted. However, several other issues need to be considered before deciding how such a shift can best be accomplished.

Career Entry and Worker Motivation

The two remaining questions that call for answers regarding government training programs are, first, what policies would be most effective in making it possible for severely disadvantaged workers to find regular, stable employment and second, what policies would contribute most to improving the motivation of such workers to find and pursue satisfying careers? These two questions are so closely related they can best be treated together.

The main thrust of the preceding chapter was that policymakers should give equal emphasis to subsidized job opportunities and subsidized job training in dealing with severely disadvantaged workers—that both of these aspects of the individual's development need to be kept in focus, if not simultaneously then certainly sequentially. The finding of the present chapter, especially in the opening section, was that this joint work-and-training conception has received little more than lip service by officials and as such constitutes the most serious gap in the government's efforts to deal effectively with the hardcore unemployed.

One of the most difficult aspects of developing stronger policies along these lines is that of reconciling the needs and expectations of the workers and employers involved, the recurring issue touched on at many points in earlier chapters. It can be safely assumed that many of the hardest-to-employ workers are those least ready to accept the discipline and standards of even entry-level jobs, much less of higher level positions. On the other hand, the reluctance on the part of even the most community spirited employers to take on workers with such serious deficiencies is to be expected whether they are subsidized or not. Experience with efforts to break through this economic-social stalemate by means of government training programs has yielded little in the way of specific guides for policymakers, but a few recommendations deserve mention.

In considering how government training programs can best be fitted into the job finding, career-development needs of workers facing the most serious barriers to steady employment, the experience under public service employment programs reviewed in the previous chapter highlights the policymaking issues involved: sorting out the individual worker's immediate job and longer term career interests; identifying the specific steps the individual would need to take to realize them; offering the training and related services required; providing the subsidized employment opportunity most likely to contribute to this outcome; and strengthening the worker's motivation by providing rewards at frequent intervals during subsidized employment.

This is obviously an idealized view of how the problem posed by severely disadvantaged workers can best be approached but its use lies in indicating the general direction government training programs will need to follow. One of the key considerations is to make sure workers engage in training that has meaning in terms of their particular interests and prospects. Training for the sake of training may provide a temporary kind of support but can hardly lay the basis for longer term benefits; the training has to be part of some career plan, however modest and limited, to enlist a worker's genuine involvement. At the same time, the training has to be structured in such a way that the individual sees quite immediate and concrete advantages in performing satisfactorily. This would mean breaking up the training into a series of well-defined steps with periodic evaluations and income adjustments at each stage.

On first consideration, an approach to government training programs along these individualized, intensive lines would seem hopelessly impractical. It is important to remember, however, that the most severely disadvantaged group, as defined in this study, comes to no more than 500,000 to 750,000 workers in the country as a whole, so in any given locality, the number would be comparatively small. More important, within this group a considerable portion could doubtless be assigned to relatively specific, short term training opportunities. Even narrowly defined, the severely disadvantaged constitute a wide diversity of abilities, motivations and outlooks, and for a significant number, a relatively brief period of training supplemented by only one or two related services could well prove sufficient.

The other key consideration is the response on the part of employers to this type of government training, not only during the period of subsidization but afterwards as well. As emphasized earlier, the active cooperation of both private and public employers is essential to the success of any such program, but their cooperation cannot be expected unless they have adequate knowledge about the abilities and related qualities of workers in the program. No set of procedures can fully provide this information in every instance, but a system of periodic evaluations of each participant's progress would surely help. Such a system, if properly designed, could be extremely useful in enlisting the active support of employers as well as providing a continuing incentive to the workers to move ahead in the program.

This view of the role of government training programs parallels the approach to public service employment developed in the preceding chapter with the two functions closely integrated with one another. Whether in a given instance, training or job experience should receive major emphasis would depend on such factors as the participant's prior work history, educational level, degree of job readiness and general background. In most cases a rough kind of balancing would probably be appropriate with somewhat greater emphasis on one or the other at different phases of an individual's work and training.

Two national programs present striking contrasts in this regard: the Supported Work Demonstration project, which is primarily limited to work experience, and the Job Corps program, which is primarily limited to job training.[9] On average, the Supported Work participants spend slightly over 80 percent of their program days on work projects while Corps members spend somewhat less than 27 percent of their time on work activities. The other major difference between the two programs is that the Job Corps is largely a residential program and involves placing severely disadvantaged young men and women age 14-21 in urban and rural training centers away from their home and neighborhood environments. Both programs, nonetheless, follow the same approach in that participants receive comprehensive services on an intensive basis which it is hoped will subsequently enable them to find steady jobs in the regular labor market.

Experience under these two ambitious programs does not point unequivocally to one being superior to the other. With respect to young participants alone, the age groups which make up all those served by Job Corps but which constitutes only one of the four groups in the Supported Work project, neither program can be said to be a clear success. As in-

---

9. Manpower Research Demonstration Corporation, *Summary of Findings of the National Supported Work Demonstration* and Mathematica Policy Research, *A Comparative Evaluation of the Benefits and Costs of the Job Corps After Seven Months of Postprogram Follow-Up,* Office of Youth Programs Report No. 10 (Washington: U.S. Department of Labor, February, 1979).

dicated in the preceding chapter, the sampling of the youth target group in the Supported Work program was no more successful in subsequently finding jobs than their control group counterparts. Participants in the Job Corps, on the other hand, were achieving roughly 10 percent higher earnings seven months after leaving the program than non-enrollees. The principal difficulty confronting Job Corps is its poor retention rate: the average length of stay is only a little over 5.5 months, with the rate declining from 5.9 months in 1977 to 5.6 months in 1978. The economic and noneconomic benefits of the Job Corps experience are directly related to the length of time an enrollee remains in the Corps. Thus only 65.6 percent of terminees who were in the Job Corps 4 to 6 months found jobs in fiscal 1978 and their starting wage was $3.06 per hour, while the employment rate for those in the program over 15 months was 79.5 percent and their starting wage was $3.47 per hour. A closely related problem is the poor record with respect to placement of terminees in jobs; in fiscal 1978, only 27 percent had full time jobs seven months after leaving the program, though 68 percent reported they had entered some kind of employment that year. More disturbing still, the record shows that only one of seven Corps members who enters the vocational training program ends up completing it and being placed, upon termination, in a job in the same cluster.[10]

As in the case of the Job Corps the Supported Work program achieved its greatest success with those participants who saw specific gains from doing well in the program and placed high value on realizing those gains. It was AFDC mothers with family responsibilities who had the best postprogram record in finding jobs in the study of the four

10. *Employment and Training Report of the President, 1979,* pp. 120-174 and 179-182; Mathematica Policy Research, *A Comparative Evaluation of the Benefits and Costs of the Job Corps After Seven Months of Postprogram Follow-Up,* Office of Youth Programs Report No. 10 (Washington: U.S. Department of Labor, February 1979).

Supported Work groups noted in the preceding chapter, followed by the ex-addict group. The two remaining groups, young school dropouts and ex-offenders released from custody, had the poorest postprogram employment experiences. Both of these groups, it is worth noting, represented a relatively broad spectrum of work attitudes and general outlooks. Viewed in these terms, it appears that the most serious impediment to effective government action in dealing with unemployment among severely disadvantaged workers is the inability to establish adequate incentives that would induce the steps necessary to qualify for work in the regular market.

This leaves the critical question of employer response and cooperation still to be considered. Put in terms of incentives, the answer to this question turns on what inducements and circumstances would prove most effective in gaining employer participation. As developed earlier, formidable barriers stand in the way of achieving employer acceptance of workers from severely disadvantaged backgrounds, barriers that are just as much the product of long-standing social attitudes as more strictly economic considerations. One of the most promising approaches to stronger employer participation is to provide monetary incentives which will at the very least give added strength to other inducements working in this direction. Unfortunately, little is known of a systematic nature about this issue, but whatever route is taken, it seems likely that some type of wage subsidy system will be adopted. A review of the general principles that would underlie such a system would therefore seem appropriate.

Chapter 10
Wage Subsidies and Employment
James R. Knickman*

A particularly disturbing component of unemployment is that found among low wage, unskilled workers. This unemployment, which is significantly more common than joblessness among higher wage workers, is especially serious because of the chronic difficulty of effectively decreasing the permanent rate of unemployment experienced by this sector of the labor market.[1]

In 1977 Congress passed legislation designed to increase private employment of low paid workers by providing tax credits over the following two years to employers who hired more of such workers.[2] This was to be achieved by granting

---

*Assistant Professor, Graduate School of Public Administration, New York University.

1. One method for determining unemployment rates for low wage workers versus high wage workers is to compare unemployment rates for demographic groups that are known to have varying average wage rates. For instance, in the third quarter of 1977, when the overall unemployment rate was 10 percent, the unemployment rates for adult blacks, teenage blacks, and white teenagers, three groups with lower than average wage rates were 11.1 percent, 39.5 percent, and 15 percent, respectively. White males, between 25 and 55, by contrast, had an unemployment rate of 3.7 percent. These figures are from Lester Thurow, "Inequality, Inflation and Growth in The American Economy," *The Economist* (December 24, 1977).

2. The summary of existing legislation is based on the testimony of Arnold H. Packer, Assistant Secretary for Policy, Evaluation and Research, U.S. Department of Labor, before the Subcommittee on Administration of the Internal Revenue Code, Committee on Finance and the Select Committee on Small Business, U.S. Senate, July 18, 1978.

employers credits equal to 50 percent of any increase in a firm's federal unemployment tax wage base over 102 percent of the previous year's base. Thus, a firm hiring an additional worker could receive 50 percent of the worker's first $4,200 of earnings as a tax credit. The legislation set a ceiling of $100,000 on the amount of tax credits that could be received by any one firm in a given year. Limiting the credits to the first $4,200 of earnings meant that the percentage subsidy would be higher for low wage than for high wage workers.

Earlier, in 1971, Congress had passed similar legislation, subsequently amended in 1975, 1976 and 1977, providing tax credits to employers who hired enrollees in the Work Incentive (WIN) and other welfare programs. Under this legislation employers could claim 20 percent of the first year wages of eligible workers. Both the WIN and welfare credits required minimum duration periods of employment. Employers also were restricted from laying off or reducing the hours of other workers eligible for the credits, and the maximum an employer could claim for any one tax year was $50,000 plus one-half of tax liability over $50,000.

The chief policy question posed by any tax credit or subsidy scheme is how much reliance should be placed on this approach to reducing unemployment among low wage workers. If the goal is to increase employment among such workers by a million or more, a very substantial liberalization of the tax credit and eligibility provisions of the 1977 legislation would be required. A program along these lines suggested by Robert Eisner, for example, could be expected to incur a gross tax cost to the Treasury of as much as $20 billion compared to $2.4 billion projected for 1978 under the present program.[3] An effort of this dimension would mean

---

3. Robert Eisner, "A Direct Attack on Unemployment and Inflation," *Challenge* (July-August 1978), pp. 49-51. Allowance for savings on unemployment benefits and other income maintenance expenditures as well as for increases in tax receipts from the increased employment would cut the gross tax cost by as much as a half.

that the government has shifted from broad expansionary measures such as across-the-board tax cuts to a selective expansionary program aimed primarily at creating jobs for low wage workers in the private sector. The Carter administration has favored some action along the latter lines but not to the point of supplanting or even materially reducing broad expansionary measures; in fact, it has proposed to narrow the focus of the job tax credit program sharply by limiting it largely to disadvantaged youth between 18 and 24 years of age.[4]

In this chapter, a general analysis of the likely labor market impacts of a wage subsidy is presented. The impacts that could be expected on the supply of low wage labor, the demand for low wage labor, and the rates of employment and unemployment are each discussed.

Types and Effects

Wage subsidies can take two forms: a subsidy paid directly to the employer based on the number of hours worked by low wage employees or a subsidy paid directly to the employee. In the latter case, a target wage is selected and then the government pays a subsidy that equals some percentage of the difference between the earned wage of the worker and the target wage. This subsidy is paid on each hour worked by the individual.[5]

Kesselman has shown that the two forms of the wage subsidy have identical labor market effects if the subsidy is paid to or for every worker earning less than the preset target wage.[6] If the subsidy is categorical in that only a subset of

4. See Packer, testimony before the Subcommittee on Administration.

5. For example, if a target wage of $4 is set and the wage subsidy is to pay 50 percent of the difference between earned wage and the $4 target wage, then an individual who earns $3 per hour would receive a subsidy of $.50 per hour (50 percent x [$4-$3] = $.50). Similarly a person earning $2 per hour would receive a $1 per hour subsidy.

6. Jonathan Kesselman, "Labor Supply Effects of Income, Income-Work, and Wage Subsidies," *Journal of Human Resources* (Summer 1969).

low wage workers is eligible for the subsidy, then the two forms of the subsidy can have very different labor market effects. For example, a categorical wage subsidy paid to employers would likely cause employers to substitute eligible workers for ineligible workers (if their skills were the same) whereas this response is not as likely if the subsidy is paid to the employee directly.

Studies of wage subsidies in the past have focused predominantly on the antipoverty effects of this public policy.[7] To the extent that total wages (earned wage plus subsidy) increase for subsidy recipients, a wage subsidy program would increase the income of the working poor, a group largely ignored by the current income support system.

In the following pages we focus on the potential employment and unemployment effects of a wage subsidy. Specifically, we are interested in whether or not a wage subsidy would create more jobs for low wage, unskilled workers and how such a program would likely affect the measured rate of unemployment. A wage subsidy paid to workers will be considered first, followed by a short discussion of the likely effects of a wage subsidy paid to employers.

The Effect of Subsidies Paid to Employees on the Aggregate Level of Employment

To determine a wage subsidy's effects on employment, it is necessary to determine both its impact on the supply of labor and on the demand for labor. If the subsidy is paid to the employee, demand can be affected only if the subsidy first changes the total amount of labor supplied.

---

7. For examples of this literature, see Kesselman, "Labor Supply Effects" and John Bishop, *The General Equilibrium Impact of Alternative Antipoverty Strategies,* Institute for Research on Poverty Discussion Paper No. 386-77, February 1977.

The labor supply response is likely to differ across varying subgroups of the low wage labor market. Specifically, the labor supply of teenagers and women has been found to be more responsive to wage changes than the labor supply of prime age males.[8]

In estimating the labor supply effects for prime age males, it is important to distinguish between aggregate and micro effects. Econometric studies have added weight to the hypothesis that employed, prime age males decrease their work effort, on average, as their wages increase.[9] Effectively, the studies show that men who have jobs use the extra income resulting from a wage increase to "buy" extra leisure time. They can earn as much (or perhaps more) income after the wage increase even if they work fewer total hours.[10] These studies use disaggregated cross section data in confirming the existence of a "backward bending" individual labor supply curve.

The results do not imply, however, that the total amount of labor supplied at a given wage by all males in that wage class will decrease if the wage rate increases. An influx of former nonworkers into the labor force and the employment of workers formerly unemployed could more than make up for the decrease in annual hours among those actually working before the wage increases. In three studies which accounted for changes in labor force participation along with changes in annual hours by those working, positive total

8. See Glen Cain and Harold Watts, eds., *Income Maintenance and Labor Supply* (New York: Academic Press, 1973).

9. Ibid.

10. Wage changes cause both price (or substitution) effects and income effects on work hours. Labor supply studies indicate that the negative income effect is larger than the positive substitution effect for males.

labor supply curves resulted from cross section disaggregated estimation.[11]

If males who have jobs reduce their total hours of work in response to a wage increase, jobs in the low wage labor market may be created just to keep aggregate labor supply as high as it was before the wage subsidy. Thus one wage subsidy result, even if aggregate demand was unaffected, would be more individuals working with work hours per male lower than before the implementation of the wage subsidy.

Studies of labor supply among women and teenagers generally find a positive effect of wage increases on labor supplied by these groups at both the individual and aggregate level. Women and teenagers who hold jobs tend to increase their work hours when wage rates increase and, in addition, some nonworkers accept employment when wages increase. Thus, a wage subsidy would unambiguously increase the aggregate labor supply of women and teenagers.

From a supply perspective, therefore, the likely impact of a wage subsidy paid to employees would be:

(1) an increase in the total number of workers offering labor services in the low wage labor market,
(2) a decrease in the average hours worked among male workers who held jobs prior to the wage subsidy, and
(3) an increase in average work hours among women and teenagers who held jobs prior to the wage subsidy.

The net impact of these three supply responses would be an increase in aggregate labor supply among low wage workers. This increase would likely cause the market wage

11. See Edward Kalacheck and Frederic Raines, "Labor Supply of Low Income Workers," Technical Studies, The President's Commission on Income Maintenance Programs (Washington: Government Printing Office, 1970); Robert Hall, "Wages, Income, and Hours of Work in the U.S. Labor Force," in Cain and Watts, eds., *Income Maintenance and Labor Supply;* and C. Russell Hill, "The Determinants of Labor Supply for the Working Urban Poor," in Cain and Watts, eds., *Income Maintenance and Labor Supply.*

rate to fall and, therefore, the demand for labor to increase. This assumes that the elasticity of demand for low wage labor is negative as has been documented in most studies of labor demand.[12]

Barth has simulated the impact of a wage subsidy on employment demand and supply with a simple three equation supply and demand model.[13] For various possible values of aggregate supply and demand elasticities, he computes the employment effects of a program with a target wage of $3.00 per hour and a subsidy rate of 50 percent.[14] His results indicate that employment would increase by 3.05 percent if the demand elasticity is -.4 and the supply elasticity is +.2. This employment effect is larger if either the actual supply or demand elasticity is in fact larger than -.4 or +.2.

Bishop designed a more complex simulation model that accounts for substitutability of low and high wage labor in the production process and allows for occupational mobility among workers.[15] Although his results are not reported in the same form as those of Barth, Bishop does note that his results indicate that Barth's simpler model understates the employment effects of a wage subsidy.

These results suggest that a wage subsidy policy would increase employment in the low wage labor market. The results do not determine, however, whether this increased employ-

---

12. See Daniel Hamermesh, "Econometric Studies of Labor Demand and Their Application to Policy Analysis," *Journal of Human Resources* (Fall 1976) for a review of these demand studies.

13. Michael Barth, "Market Effects of a Wage Subsidy," *Industrial and Labor Relations Review,* Vol. 27, 1974. The three equations in Barth's model are a demand equation, a supply equation, and an identity that sets demand equal to supply.

14. Barth uses data from the 1967 Survey of Economic Opportunity. A wage subsidy, if implemented in 1980, would obviously have a substantially higher target wage than $3 per hour reflecting high price and wage levels.

15. John Bishop, "Impact of Antipoverty Strategies."

ment would come from those who are unemployed during a period of full employment or from those who are not in the labor force prior to the wage subsidy. It seems likely, however, that at least part of the employment increase would be composed of formerly unemployed workers and formerly "discouraged" workers who had given up looking for work and thus were not counted as being unemployed.

Effects of a Wage Subsidy Paid to Employers on Aggregate Level of Employment

Rather than paying subsidies directly to employees, a wage subsidy program could make payments to low wage employers. This type of program is often called a wage bill subsidy. In essence, such a program would be analogous to investment credit programs that use tax credits to subsidize the use of capital. A significant advantage of a program that pays subsidies to employers is that the subsidies could be targeted at specific demographic groups that are characterized by high unemployment rates. Thus, for example, the program could be designed to pay subsidies only if teenagers were hired or, alternatively, only if household heads were hired.

Thurow argues that such a wage bill subsidy strategy is the most viable approach to decreasing unemployment rates among low skilled workers in an economy where unemployment rates differ across demographic and skill groups.[16] Most other unemployment strategies cause a good deal of inflation in such an economy, according to Thurow.

A subsidy paid only to employers of selected demographic and skill groups would likely lead to increased employment among these groups for two reasons: first, the cost of this type of labor would decrease, thus making it efficient to pro-

---

16. Lester Thurow, "Inequality, Inflation, and Growth."

duce more output using extra amounts of the subsidized labor; and second, subsidized labor would be substituted for unsubsidized labor because of the change in the relative prices of the two categories of labor.

It is not clear that the substitution of subsidized labor for unsubsidized labor would increase aggregate employment levels. It is likely that unemployment would merely decrease among groups of individuals eligible for a subsidy while unemployment would increase for nonsubsidized workers.

To the extent that output increases and labor demand increases due to a wage bill subsidy, however, employment should increase in the low wage labor market. The magnitude of employment effects due to the decreased cost of subsidized labor depend on labor supply and labor demand elasticities in the same manner as does the magnitude of employment effects related to wage subsidies paid directly to workers. The total increase in employment due to a wage bill subsidy will be smaller than the estimate presented in the last section to the extent that the wage bill subsidy is categorical and pays subsidies only to a portion of the low wage labor market. As mentioned before, if a wage bill subsidy applies to all low wage workers, then the employment effects of subsidies paid to employers are identical to the effects of subsidies paid to employees.

Effects of a Wage Subsidy on the Measured Rate of Permanent Unemployment

Besides expanding the number of low wage jobs, a wage subsidy paid to the employee or the employer may also have an impact on the number of unemployment spells that the average low wage worker experiences. To predict a wage subsidy's effect on the measured rate of unemployment, however, the causes of unemployment in the low wage labor market must be identified.

One hypothesis for the cause of low wage unemployment is offered by the dual or segmented labor market theory which suggests that much of low wage joblessness in times of full employment can be viewed as a type of frictional unemployment.[17] Low wage workers change jobs frequently because their low wage makes the cost of job search minimal.[18] The existence of various welfare programs and nonlegal or other nonreported work opportunities reduces further the costs of taking time off.

As a result of this low return on labor, workers quit their jobs frequently, continually moving into and out of the labor force. At any point in time a certain number of individuals are attempting to move back into the labor force or to find jobs, having recently left other low wage jobs. These job seekers are counted as unemployed. Evidence indicates that the average duration of an unemployment spell is shorter for low wage than high wage workers,[19] and that in times of full employment jobs are available although they might not be desirable opportunities.[20]

These unemployment spells, therefore, cannot be traced to deficient demand but rather are caused by a divergence of the wage return offered by available jobs and the wage return desired by the unemployed individual. If the wage offer reflects the actual marginal productivity of the "searching" worker, then the worker, after a finite, unsuccessful search, will either accept the low wage offer or leave the

17. See Peter Doeringer and Michael J. Piore, *Internal Labor Markets and Manpower Analysis* (Lexington, MA: D.C. Heath , 1971) for a good survey of the segmented labor market theory. See especially ch. 8.

18. Modern Job Search Theory emphasizes the need to take a spell of joblessness in order to look for a better job. See *Microeconomic Foundations of Employment and Inflation Theory* (New York: Norton, 1970), edited by Edmund S. Phelps et al.

19. See George Perry, "Unemployment Flows in the Labor Market."

20. See Peter Doeringer, ed., *Low Income Labor Markets and Urban Manpower Programs* (Springfield, VA: National Technical Information Service, 1969).

labor force in favor of public assistance or nonlegal earning opportunities.[21]

Segmented labor market theorists argue that this instability of labor supply has caused employers to structure jobs to accommodate frequent turnover. Low wage jobs are designed so that little or no training is necessary, few work responsibilities are given to the workers, and the normal incentives of advancement through an "internal labor market" are not offered to these workers. This structuring of jobs, in turn, results in boring, unappealing work conditions and causes even more quitting and instability of labor supply.

The process is dynamic, with the chain of causation often blurred. It seems clear, however, that an important link in this circular chain is the high quit rate prevalent in the low wage labor market. To the extent that the wage subsidy reduces the quit rate and increases stability of supply, the other characteristics of the low wage labor market should improve.

Numerous studies have shown that quit rates are negatively related to wage rates. Ulman has shown that quit rates in low wage industries are significantly higher than in high wage industries.[22] Severn[23] and Armknecht and Early[24] came

21. An implied assumption in this analysis is that the desirability of a job is completely reflected in the wage rate of the job. This is a standard assumption in economic theory, but not so clear from surveying actual jobs. Besides work conditions, however, the wage also reflects the training, education, and skills required of the job. The fact that low wage jobs look so unattractive can be explained by the fact that the amount of training or skills required for a job seems to be positively correlated with the perceived attractiveness of jobs. This does not contradict the assumption that undesirable or more difficult jobs within the unskilled class of jobs have higher wages than more desirable jobs.

22. Lloyd Ulman, "Labor Mobility and the Industrial Wage," *Quarterly Journal of Economics,* Vol. 79, 1965.

23. Alan Severn, "Upward Labor Mobility" *Quarterly Journal of Economics,* Vol. 82, 1968.

24. Paul Armknecht and John Early, "Quits in Manufacturing: A Study of Their Causes," *Monthly Labor Review,* November 1972.

to similar conclusions, showing that the relation between an individual's quit rate and the interindustrial relative wage is negative. Hall argues that the frequency of low wage unemployment is due to high turnover among unskilled workers.[25]

Thus, one can tentatively expect that a wage subsidy, which increases the net wage paid to individuals, will result in less frequent turnover in the low wage labor market.[26] Effectively, the wage subsidy increases the wage return to a level that is closer to that desired by the low wage worker while leaving unchanged the wage paid by the employer. As a result, search becomes more costly and the return on search decreases because the relative wage differences between low wage and higher wage jobs tightens.

Any reduction in the quit rate among low wage workers could be expected to have numerous beneficial effects on the employment situation in this market. Primary among these improvements is that the increased stability of the low wage labor market should lead employers to invest in training and to restructure the work done by low wage workers so that the jobs are a part of the primary labor market. These changes could reverse the dynamic process in that a better structuring of jobs would have an independent negative effect on the quit rate and lead to further employment improvements in this labor market.

---

25. Robert Hall, *Why is the Unemployment Rate So High at Full Employment,* Brookings Papers on Economic Activity, 3 (1970).

26. The prediction must be tentative because the empirical results were obtained with aggregated, industry-wide data. A micro study of the quit rate-wage relation has never been reported, probably due to the scarcity of longitudinal survey data with accurate measures of voluntary separations. A micro study would allow for more control of other socioeconomic factors that may affect quit rates. It is possible that such factors are correlated with wage rates, and that the aggregate studies may therefore overestimate the negative wage effect on quit rates.

The above conclusions are based on a specific theory of low wage labor market processes. This theory is a segmented labor market theory which emphasizes characteristics of labor *supply* as the cause of the undesirable labor market structure in full employment periods. In contrast, other explanations of low wage unemployment have emphasized demand factors in this labor market. It may be argued that demand for low wage labor is very unstable, either due to seasonality of work or the importance of favorable (and often cyclical) market conditions for profits in many low wage industries. It may also be true that the nature of the work is such that no training is necessary. One other possible explanation of the secondary labor market is based on racial discrimination. Minority groups, according to this theory, are largely restricted to the secondary labor market because other groups do not want to work with them.

To the extent that the structure of the low wage labor market is the result of unstable demand and racial discrimination, wage subsidies cannot be expected to change the structure of jobs. Unfortunately, neither empirical studies nor informed opinions have pinpointed the amount of accountability for the structure of the secondary labor market attributable to each of the three causal factors discussed above.

One final explanation for chronically high unemployment rates in the low wage labor market is the existence of social minimum wages and the development of varying wages among different firms for jobs requiring the same skill level.[27] Social minimum wages are wages that are above the level required to ensure needed labor supplies. Some

27. Wage differentials within the unskilled labor market may also result from differences in wages paid by competitive and noncompetitive firms. For a recent formulation of this wage differential hypothesis, see Steven Ross and Michael Wachter, "Wage Determination, Inflation, and the Industrial Structure," *American Economic Review* (September 1973).

employers pay this "above equilibrium" wage because of their desire to pay a "fair" wage and to avoid accusations that they pay "slave wages." If social minimum wages are paid by some but not all low wage employers, a wage differential within the unskilled labor market develops. This differential increases the return on job search. Thus, for instance, workers may quit a low paying unskilled job to find a "premium" wage unskilled job, such as a construction laborer, a mail carrier, or a garbage collector. Many such jobs, which require no special skills, exist and pay better than other less attractive, unskilled jobs.

As long as the social minimum wage exceeds the subsidized wage, a wage subsidy should not alter these social minimum wage levels. The wage subsidy, however, would narrow the gap between the wages paid by competitive firms and those paid by social minimum wage firms. This would decrease the return on job search and should result in less voluntary turnover and, therefore, less measured unemployment in the low wage labor market.

Potential Problems of the Wage Subsidy

The predominant wage effect of a wage subsidy will be to homogenize the level of wages paid to unskilled workers earning less than the target wage. Postsubsidy wages will vary less than presubsidy wages. This homogenization of low wages might act to discourage job advancement. Just as the return for job search is decreased, the return on training and education will decrease because a $1.00 increase in market wage will result in a ($1.-r) increase in net wage, where r is the subsidy rate. This argument is valid only if job advancement is determined by the actual net wage differential.

If it is valid to view the labor market as a ladder of increasingly higher paying jobs and if passage to the highest paying jobs is only possible by proceeding one rung at a time, then the return on advancing from one job to another is not only the actual net wage differential but also the long term potential gains of moving further up the job ladder.

Also, if we consider jobs paying below the target wage to be exclusively in the "secondary" labor market, no advancement disincentives will occur in the primary internal labor markets where most job advancement actually occurs. Thus, although the wage subsidy does have a negative effect on job improvement incentives, it is not clear how disruptive this effect, which is limited only to the relative wages in the lowest wage category, will be on overall advancement incentives.

The homogenization of low wages also may lead to some undesirable market results. Firms operating in expanding product markets signal their needs for additional labor by paying a higher than equilibrium wage. Labor flows from firms in other markets to the expanding firms until the nonexpanding firms reestablish the equality of wages. This process ensures efficient flows of labor from declining to expanding industries. With the presence of wage subsidies, an expanding firm would have to raise the market wage by a larger amount than in the absence of wage subsidies in order to significantly change the net wage of workers so that they will change jobs and so that additional labor supply will be forthcoming. This may result in a less adaptable and, therefore, more inefficient economy.

A third shortcoming of the wage supplement program is the possibility that low wage labor will be used in place of higher paid skilled labor. If the market wage in the low wage market decreases, the relative price of labor will change while the relative efficiency of low versus high wage labor will remain the same. According to competitive economic theory, this should lead to a redistribution of labor inputs in favor of low wage, unskilled labor. The result would be counter to the general manpower policy goal of upgrading the level of jobs held by workers at the lower end of the wage distribution.

Conclusion

This chapter has reviewed the likely market effects of a wage subsidy program that would subsidize low wage individuals' wage rates either directly or indirectly through employers. In general, a wage subsidy would have favorable employment and unemployment effects. More individuals would supply labor to the low wage labor market, more individuals would likely find employment due to the effects of the program on labor demand, and the measured rate of unemployment might decrease if the program made low wage labor supply more stable. Potential problems of a wage subsidy program include the possibility that the homogenization of wage rates in the low wage market will impede labor mobility and the likelihood that the program would weaken the demand for skilled labor due to the substitution of subsidized manpower for nonsubsidized manpower.

Chapter 11
Conclusion

This study has focused on the role of government in reducing the level of unemployment in periods of high employment. While differing in degree, the same three aspects of unemployment—cyclical, frictional and structural—must be addressed in periods of high as in periods of low employment. In both environments the most difficult issue to resolve is how to mesh short-run and long-run goals for the economy in choosing among public policy alternatives. When labor markets are generally loose, major emphasis shifts to short-run expansionary measures in aggregate demand. Even then, however, account has to be taken of possible longer run destablizing consequences of such measures. Moreover, despite the shift in emphasis, the need to deal with both the frictional and structural aspects of unemployment is still present in periods of general slack and, considered in this light, essentially the same policy measures are called for as in periods of high employment.

Similar considerations apply in periods of prosperity. The unemployment which persists into such periods is predominantly frictional and structural in nature and calls for greater emphasis on longer run policies pertaining to supply allocation issues than when labor markets are looser. Nonetheless, there are important differences between individual periods of prosperity, as recent experience makes

187

clear, so short-run shifts in demand management must still be held in readiness. Moreover, not all aspects of frictional and structural unemployment call for long term policy actions; shorter run measures, particularly with respect to demand conditions for the structurally unemployed, are clearly needed even when the economy is getting close to its full employment potential.

A profile of the unemployed by the usual demographic characteristics is also frequently viewed in terms of these same three categories of unemployment—cyclical, frictional and structural—with white adult males predominantly affected by cyclical influences, white youth and women by frictional influences, and nonwhites generally by structural influences. While containing some validity, this view is a dangerous oversimplification. It would be closer to the facts to treat the nonwhite workers as vulnerable to all three types of influences, with white youth and women only somewhat less so, and adult white males subject largely to cyclical influences alone.

As a consequence, any shift from a sluggish to a buoyant economy results in major changes in the jobless status and prospects of these demographic groups, but the degree and even the nature of the change vary among the three groups. Adult white males face increasingly active bidding for their services as vacancies multiply; substantial numbers of white youth and women begin to move into stable job opportunities and away from high turnover, structurally limited lines of work; and nonwhites begin a similar movement though to a markedly less degree.

These considerations have a direct bearing on the dimensions of the problem of prosperity unemployment as outlined in the opening chapter of this study and on the choice of public policies for dealing with the issues involved. While short-run shifts in aggregate demand management will continue to be critically important in determining how low the level of unemployment can be pushed in periods of high employment, the aggregate fiscal and monetary approach has been severely undercut in recent years by the fact that inflationary outbursts can occur at relatively high as well as at relatively low levels of unemployment. Moreover, longer term trends in economic conditions, notably the rate of growth in productivity, the pace of technological development and investment, shifts in international markets and expectations regarding the rate of increase in prices and wages, now dominate aggregate demand management. Overheating in the early phase of an expansion is quite as dangerous as overkilling later on. In today's environment, any changes in monetary and fiscal policies, barring wartime or similar shocks, will need to be kept within narrow limits.

The record of the 1970s, however, does not point to any precise nonaccelerating inflation level of unemployment to which a policy of aggregate demand expansion can be carried. All that can be said with a fair degree of assurance is that the use of such a policy to go as low as the 5 percent level might well induce serious inflationary consequences. In these circumstances, a rise in government expenditures limited to certain targeted unemployed groups would not prove unstabilizing if it were matched by an offsetting decline in some other category of spending and/or by a rise in tax revenues. This, however, would mark a shift from aggregate demand to selective measures as the route to follow. Whether the government should decide under these conditions to push unemployment below 5 percent would be as much a political as an economic choice.

The other dimension of the problem—frequent movement among unskilled, dead-end occupations, inability to secure career-oriented jobs particularly in the private sector, and lack of visible incentives to gain skills essential to more meaningful work—call for a sustained, coordinated public effort to give the hard-to-employ the means to find stable work opportunities. This would require in turn the careful tailoring of such an effort to the specific requirements of these groups, with the greatest concentration on the severely disadvantaged among the hard-to-employ. It would likewise require the careful tailoring of a system of strong inducements to employers, especially in the private sector, to give these workers initial access to career ladder jobs. While the difficulties facing both undertakings are formidable, they would be materially lessened in periods of general business expansion.

In such periods the nature of frictional unemployment undergoes considerable change as more workers, including nonwhites as well as whites and lesser as well as more skilled workers, enjoy wider latitude in choosing among job openings. For these workers, the job information facilities of the federal-state Employment Service and private employment offices, if put on a fuller, more detailed basis, should generally prove sufficient. With the step-up in business activity, employers would find it increasingly to their advantage to do more of their hiring through the Employment Service, especially if the Service's referral system could be put on a more informative, i.e., detailed, and objective basis. For a limited group of job seekers, however, the movement between jobs would remain at a bare, limited-skill level even in periods of prosperity and for these hardcore unemployed or underemployed a much more intensive, carefully designed structure of job finding aids would be essential.

Workers subject to such structural as opposed to frictional unemployment confront one or more of the following impediments: noncompetitive wages or other cost barriers, welfare assistance and other work disincentives, discriminatory hiring and promotion practices, deficiencies in basic educational and vocational preparation, and lack of any regular job experience or specific skill training.

Each of these barriers has generated public policy responses of varying degrees of intensity and effectiveness. The review of these responses in the preceding chapters underscores the need to put the different policies towards the structurally unemployed into a single, integrated framework with a view to adapting the various policy responses to the particular needs of each subgroup within the structurally unemployed and to make sure that successive-stage linkups between schools, employers and community are in place as needed by individual workers. While the underlying purpose of these policies is to make it possible for structurally unemployed workers to find and hold stable jobs, differences among such workers require distinctly different, though closely interrelated, policy approaches.

A critical element in an integrated policy framework along these lines would continue to be the government's training programs, but these programs need to be tied in much more closely than they are now with actual job experience in private firms or government agencies. Admittedly, for many workers merely providing relatively brief training and work experience opportunities of this sort has proven inadequate, but for those who have achieved a certain job-readiness status, this approach has proven highly successful; while reliable data are lacking, it seems likely that if the economy achieves a 6 percent level of unemployment, there would be as many as a million workers who, though still structurally unemployed, would be in this job-ready category. Two requirements, however, would have to be met: first, the level of training and job experience would have to be high enough to be seen as likely to lead to permanent jobs and longer term careers; and second, the inducements to both the participating workers and employers would have to be great enough to make sure that career entry and progression can occur. The single most serious weakness in existing government and public service employment sponsored programs appears to be the low rates of post-training program placements in regular, stable jobs.

Viewed in broader and more long-run terms, major changes in the nation's public school system are needed if the structural unemployment problem is to be effectively attacked. Of the various conditions that call for redress, two bear most directly on the issue of structural unemployment. The first is the gross difference that exists in terms of per student dollar outlay and comparative quality of programs between upper and lower income communities or districts. The second is the failure of the schools, notably in the latter areas, to provide meaningful work experience opportunities to students who desire them and could put them to good use. In many institutions, particularly in our inner-cities, large numbers of students find themselves on a mechanical, boring and deadening treadmill which leads away from, rather than toward, any worthwhile job or meaningful career.

For structurally unemployed workers who are less job-ready, and the more severely disadvantaged, elements other than specific skill training and work experience would also have to be provided. While primarily affecting younger workers, adult workers can be subject to essentially similar deficiencies too. These more seriously disadvantaged workers form a far smaller group, perhaps between 500,000 to 750,000 in total number, than those in the job-ready category, and thus add only about a half of a percentage point to the nation's overall unemployment rate.

A much broader, and at the same time much more intensive, effort than has been expended to date would be necessary if any significant progress is to be made in their case. Training periods would have to be lengthened, work support assignments would have to be more carefully designed and monitored, more individual counseling and help with personal needs would have to be made available, and during initial job assignments, much fuller, even daily, cooperation of supervisors and fellow workers would have to be secured.

Even if such an intensive effort could be carried through, however, only limited results would probably be achieved, with numerous outright failures occurring since for many such workers these aids would not reach the fundamental difficulties involved. In their case, in addition to these direct, individualized measures, much broader and more costly measures would have to be undertaken including, in some instances at least, greatly improved housing conditions, far better crime control, more adequate recreational facilities and other like measures essential to viable neighborhood and community environments. As already indicated, a key element in any such far-reaching effort would be to adapt the country's primary and secondary school system more fully to the needs of disadvantaged students generally and, through a parallel program in work experience education, to give them some kind of a future career foothold. This would be especially important for students from the most severely disadvantaged backgrounds. Lacking a sustained effort along these lines, the many opportunities which high employment conditions afford even workers of severely disadvantaged backgrounds are likely to be largely lost.

The other major barriers involve even more difficult and intractable issues, so much so that insofar as structural unemployment is concerned they can only be approached in very long range terms. Noncompetitive wages, including government determined federal minimum wages and other market interferences, potentially pose real threats to job seekers among the hard-to-employ but, practicalities aside, whether a concerted move to break down these market barriers would have an observable effect on the employment of such workers seems doubtful. Similarly, it is important to take steps to prevent a weakening of work incentives of lower paid, lower skilled groups as a result of the spread of welfare programs and other income support systems, but there is little evidence that any such tightening would materially affect the extent of unemployment, structural or otherwise. Finally, there is wide agreement that discriminatory practices, many rooted in long-established mores and institutional patterns, lie behind many of the more specific barriers confronting the structurally unemployed. There is no less widespread agreement that the task of breaking down these practices will be long and arduous. Ultimately, any solution of the structural unemployment problem will require unremitting efforts in this direction; meanwhile, the more direct attacks already discussed give greater promise of success.

Can the level of unemployment that persists into periods of prosperity be reduced to minimal proportions, as low perhaps as 5 percent or less, in the next five or ten years? No one can speak with assurance on this question; if substantial progress is made, however, it seems likely that it will come as a result of public policy actions along the general lines recommended in this study.